THE
WHITELEY HOMES TRUST
1907-77

The founder, Mr William Whiteley.

THE WHITELEY HOMES TRUST

1907~77

Alan Brown

Phillimore

1992

Published by
PHILLIMORE & CO. LTD.
Shopwyke Hall, Chichester, Sussex

ISBN 0 85033 849 2

Printed and bound in Great Britain by
BIDDLES LTD.
Guildford, Surrey

CONTENTS

LIST OF ILLUSTRATIONS

Frontispiece: William Whiteley

FOREWORD

The life story of William Whiteley is told in the inscription on the south side of the central monument in the village which bears his name:

William Whiteley, the founder of this Trust, was born at Agbrigg, Yorks., on 29 September, 1831 educated at Pontefract and apprenticed at the age of 16 to a drapery firm in Wakefield. He went to London to see the Great Exhibition of 1851, and the busy life of the Metropolis attracted him. He spent ten years of thrift and constant study with a City firm, and then started a small business of his own at 63 Westbourne Grove. Before very long he had won for himself the name of 'The Universal Provider', and for his business a world-wide reputation. He was the pioneer of the great London retail stores of the 19th and 20th centuries. He died in London on 24 January 1907.

PREFACE

WHITELEY VILLAGE stands today as a lasting memorial to its founder, William Whiteley. This is the story of that village – of its foundation, of its building, and of those entrusted with the running of its affairs. It is also a story which tells of Mr Whiteley's true memorial – the peace, comfort and security which his foresight and generosity have given to so many old people in their retirement.

ACKNOWLEDGMENTS

Numerous people have given me help, encouragement and advice in the production of this small book, and I am grateful to them all. In particular, I should like to thank:

My wife, who spent many hours checking the script, and who made many helpful suggestions which have improved the clarity of my work;

Lady Hanworth, a Trustee since 1948, who put at my disposal her deep knowledge of all things to do with the village, and who gave me much encouragement, together with a lot of sound practical advice about the script, which she painstakingly proof-read and corrected for me;

Miss Mary Ryan, then a history student at, and now a graduate of, St Mary's College at Strawberry Hill, Twickenham, who came for part of her summer vacation for three years running to help me research the Trust's records, and without whose skilled and invaluable help I could not have written this book.

PROLOGUE

(The following is an extract from *The Universal Provider*, a biography of William Whiteley by Richard S. Lambert, and is reproduced by kind permission of the publishers and copyright holders, Harrap Ltd.).

Shortly after midday on 24th January 1907, a young man entered Lancaster Gate Tube Station, on the Central London Railway, deposited a small parcel in the cloakroom, and, having left the station, walked rapidly in the direction of Westbourne Grove. He was about twenty-seven years of age, of medium height, slim in build, clean-shaven, and of fair complexion — altogether a handsome young man, except for an odd staring look in his eyes. He was well dressed in a frockcoat and silk hat, and was obviously well educated and a gentleman. At about half-past twelve he knocked at the door of No 31 Porchester Terrace and inquired for Mr William Whiteley. The door was answered by the butler, who informed the visitor that Whiteley was out, being at his place of business in Westbourne Grove, less than a quarter of a mile from the house. Upon receiving this answer the young man went away, and a few minutes later entered the premises of the Universal Provider and repeated the request he had made at Porchester Terrace. As he did not give his name or business he was directed to a desk in No 43 Westbourne Grove, where sat Daniel Goodman, the chief cashier, who asked whether he had an appointment. The young man replied 'No', but added that he had come from Sir George Lewis, and that if Goodman would mention this fact to Mr Whiteley the latter would see him. Impressed by the name of this eminent lawyer, whose managing clerk he took the visitor to be (as a matter of fact Sir George Lewis had on several occasions acted for Whiteley in the management of his private affairs) the cashier took the message in to Whiteley's private office, and returned with instructions to admit the young man. Goodman therefore carried out his instructions, and saw Whiteley greet his caller without any appearance of recognition, and wave him in his usual affable manner to a seat before closing the door of the office.

It was the concluding week of the January sale; the shops were thronged with customers, and business was active. Whiteley was at all times accessible to visitors, but it was his rule to allow no more than five minutes interview to a casual caller. Moreover, he always lunched punctually at one o'clock, and used without fail to emerge from his room a few minutes before the hour for that purpose. It was therefore a matter of some surprise that this particular interview should have lasted nearly half an hour without interruption, except from a correspondence clerk who entered the room with some papers during its course, only to be told by Whiteley, 'I can't see you now; I hope to see you presently'. At four minutes past one, however, the door of the office was suddenly flung open, and the Universal Provider emerged from his room, evidently not in his usual state of affability and calm. He looked pale and agitated, and at once called out to one of his assistants to go out and fetch a policeman – presumably for the purpose of ridding himself of his visitor. Before this order could be carried out, however, the latter appeared behind Whiteley in the door of the office, and attempted to reopen a conversation that had evidently been going on between them.

'Won't you come in again?' asked the young man.

'No, no!' replied Whiteley. 'Go away! If you don't I shall fetch a policeman'.

'Aren't you going to come back?' asked the young man excitedly. 'Is that your final word?'

'Yes'.

'Then you are a dead man, Mr. Whiteley' – and with those words the mysterious visitor drew a revolver from his left breast pocket, presented it close to Whiteley's head, and fired two shots. The first penetrated his victim's left cheek, the second entered his head behind the right ear and proved immediately fatal. The old man, now in his seventy-sixth year, reeled and fell to the ground, where life became extinct before anyone could reach him.

Mr Whiteley's murderer was Horace George Rayner, an impoverished and unstable young man who believed himself to be Whiteley's illegitimate son. Being desperate for money, it seems that he approached Whiteley, declared that he was his son, and asked for or demanded financial help. On being refused, he killed Whiteley and then turned the gun on himself. He survived his attempted suicide, however, and when he recovered stood trial for murder. He pleaded insanity, but was nevertheless found guilty and sentenced to death. On the recommendation of the Home Secretary his sentence was reduced to penal servitude for life; but Rayner was released from prison in 1919, having served only 12 years.

Chapter One

THE FOUNDATION OF THE WHITELEY HOMES TRUST

Mr Whiteley's funeral was held on 30 January 1907. The funeral cortège, which set out from his house at 31 Porchester Terrace at 11.30 a.m., was headed by five open carriages filled with flowers. Mr Whiteley's coffin came next, carried on an open hearse, and was followed by nearly a hundred more carriages filled with members of his family, friends and staff. The funeral service was held in Christ Church, Lancaster Gate, after which the procession made its way to Kensal Green Cemetery where he was buried in the family grave.

The family then returned to 31 Porchester Terrace for the reading of his will. During his lifetime, Mr Whiteley had been no great philanthropist, although he had occasionally helped individuals and organisations in which he had a special interest. Now, in his will dated 1904, he first of all left some small legacies of between £100 and £2,000 to various hospitals. Then he settled an annuity of £1,000 upon each of his two daughters, and left £50,000 in Trust for each of his two sons. To his wife he left nothing beyond the £2,000 per annum he had settled upon her when they were legally separated in 1882. Then followed two more substantial charitable bequests: £5,000 for 'Whiteley Christmas Gifts' to be distributed to the poor of Paddington; and £5,000 to the 'Whiteley Sports Trustees' to provide prizes to encourage cricket, football, rowing and swimming among people living within five miles of Westbourne Grove. Finally came one last bequest which was to provide his memorial – a sum 'as nearly as may be in the whole to but not exceeding the sum of £1,000,000 sterling' for the purchase of land and the erection thereon 'of buildings to be used and occupied by aged poor persons of either sex as Homes in their old age'. (The clauses governing this bequest have been extracted from Mr Whiteley's will and are reproduced in full in Appendix A.)

This was a truly enormous sum of money. In 1985 it would have been worth about £35,000,000! To take possession of it and administer it in accordance with his wishes, Mr Whiteley created a self-perpetuating Board of Trustees. The composition of this was quite complicated. In Clause 30 of his will he appointed the following eight persons as Original Trustees:

The Rt Hon and Rt Revd Arthur Foley WINNINGTON-INGRAM, PC, KCVO, DD
Lord Bishop of London

The Rt Revd Cosmo Gordon LANG, MA
Bishop Suffragan of Stepney

The Rt Hon Charles Henry MILLS
Baron Hillingdon

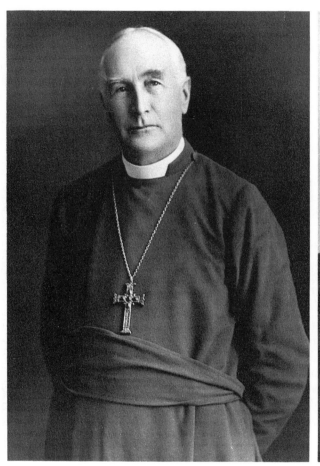

1. The Right Revd and Right Hon Arthur Foley Winnington-Ingram, PC, KCVO.

2. Cosmo Gordon Lang, Bishop of Stepney (later Archbishop of York).

The Rt Hon William MANSFIELD, GCIE
Baron Sandhurst

Sir Walpole GREENWELL Bt.,

William Edward GILLETT
Solicitor

and his two sons:

William WHITELEY and

Frank Ernest WHITELEY

3. Sir Walpole Lloyd Greenwell, Bt.   4. William Edward Gillett.

In the same Clause he gave Walpole Greenwell and William Edward Gillett the power to appoint up to three more Additional (Original) Trustees, and then, when that had been done, he gave the whole body of trustees the power to appoint such further Additional Trustees as they saw fit, without restriction as to number. However, in Clause 46 he directed that the number of trustees serving at any time should never be allowed to fall below two, and expressed the wish that it should normally be kept up to at least nine. He stipulated that if the number at any time fell below nine 'the vacancy or vacancies shall as soon as circumstances conveniently admit be filled up so as to restore that number' but he was a practical enough administrator to add that 'nevertheless any acts or proceedings of The Whiteley Homes Trustees for the time being in the interval before filling up of such vacancy or vacancies shall not be invalidated by reason of the same not having been done'. How these powers have been used over the years is shown in Appendix B, which gives a full list of trustees up to the end of 1971.

The Clauses governing this bequest contained a number of other provisions, some of which the trustees were to find difficult to fulfil and which accordingly were to lead to dissension and litigation, with inevitable delay in the setting-up of the homes. The main conditions laid down by Mr Whiteley were that:

The lands to be purchased should be of freehold tenure and situate in some or one of the western suburbs of London or in the adjacent country and if possible and convenient within 10 miles of Charing Cross.
(Clause 31)

The site to be selected ... shall be in as bright cheerful and healthy spot as possible even if such a site can only be acquired at additional expense and that in selecting such site the Whiteley Homes Trustees shall so far as may be avoid a heavy clay soil and choose a soil of gravel sand or chalk.
(Clause 31)

The buildings to be erected ... shall be of good and substantial character and of a plain and useful design and shall be well lighted, ventilated and drained and so placed as to be protected as far as possible from the north and east winds and be open to the south and west.
(Clause 33)

An outdoor shelter shall be provided.
(Clause 33)

The persons qualified to be admitted as inmates ... shall be persons of good character and of sound mind and not affected by any infectious or contagious disease and not having been convicted of any criminal offence and being male of not less than 65 years and being female of not less than 60 years of age.
(Clause 37)

Preference shall be given to persons or the wives of persons who have been engaged in commercial or agricultural pursuits.
(Clause 37)

Chapter Two

EARLY DIFFICULTIES (1907-11)

On the morning of Wednesday, 5 June 1907 the Original Trustees gathered at 32 St James's Square for their first meeting. They were all present except Baron Hillingdon who was prevented from attending by ill health. The first act of the new Trustees was to invite the Bishop of London to take the Chair, a position he was to hold for 39 years until his death in 1946.

The Trustees then went on to consider their position, and quickly came to the conclusion that, although they had thought it desirable to hold this early preliminary meeting, they were not yet in a position to take any definite steps because, firstly, the Board of Trustees as an entity would not be properly constituted until Sir Walpole Greenwell and Mr Gillett had exercised their joint power to appoint up to three more Original Trustees, and until the Board, as then constituted, had had an opportunity to exercise its collective power to appoint Additional Trustees; and secondly because, as Mr Gillett explained, the executors of the estate were not yet in a position to hand over any part of the legacy, which meant that the Trustees had as yet no funds with which to work. They were told that a very large portion of the estate consisted of shares in William Whiteley Ltd., and that the amount which the executors would eventually be able to hand over would therefore depend to a great extent upon the price which they could get when realising these shares. The stock market was at that time very depressed, and the Trustees accordingly decided '... they would not in any way hamper or endeavour to press the Executors to a hasty administration of the Estate which would be detrimental to the interests of all concerned'.

William Whiteley then told the meeting that his late father's company owned some property at Hanworth which he and his brother thought might provide a suitable site for the homes, and went on to say that as the company had received some offers for the letting of this property he would like to know whether the Trustees would wish the company to retain it unlet so that it could be made available later. This provoked considerable discussion during which a fundamental difference of opinion amongst the Trustees became apparent. On the one hand the Bishop of Stepney argued in favour of erecting a number of self-contained homes in different places on the grounds that a large number of homes concentrated on one site would not be desirable. On the other hand William and Frank Whiteley said that they thought their late father's wishes would best be met by having all the homes in one place, which would have the advantage of making them easier and more economical to run. This difference of opinion was not resolved at the first meeting, other than to agree that no decision could definitely be made about the Hanworth property.

Several of the Trustees reported that they had received requests for assistance from the Trust, and it was decided to send an announcement to the press explaining why such requests could not be met. Finally, Messrs Baileys Shaw & Gillett were requested to act as solicitors to the Trust and to obtain a minute book in which to keep the record of this and subsequent meetings.

There were two significant points to emerge from this first meeting. Firstly, there was the acceptance by the Trustees that it would be in the best long-term interest of the Trust not to hurry the executors over the realisation of the estate, as this would probably force them to do so on unfavourable terms which might result in them being unable to pay the legacy in full. Secondly, there was an early disagreement amongst the Trustees as to whether the homes should be concentrated on a single site or scattered over a number of sites, a disagreement which was to persist and which was only to be resolved by litigation.

Ten months elapsed before the Trustees met again on 7 April 1908. The main purpose of this second meeting was to hear a report from the executors about their progress with the realisation of the estate, in which they told the Trustees that, although some shares had been sold in order to meet funeral expenses, calls on shares held, and some of the smaller legacies, the period had continued to be one of unprecedented depression and stagnation on the stock exchange which had made any large realisation most undesirable. Mention was also made in the report of an impending action against the executors by the executors of J. F. Benson & Co. involving between £90,000 and £100,000 which they had been advised to defend. In the discussion which followed this report, the Trustees agreed

> ... not to interfere with the discretion of the Executors as regards the period of realisation of the Whiteley shares, at any rate at present, but it would not be right for them to fix a long period during which they would acquiesce in the delay. The question must be considered from time-to-time, but for the present they would acquiesce on the assurance of the Executors that they were watching the markets.

In the light of the financial situation the Trustees decided to postpone any further discussion about the form the homes should take, but they asked Sir Walpole Green-well and Mr Gillett to consider whom they wished to appoint to the Board under the power given them so that the Board should be complete by the time this matter next came up for consideration.

Almost another ten months elapsed before the Trustees met for the third time on 2 February 1909. This meeting began with the acceptance by the Board of the resig-nations of the Bishop of Stepney, who had been preferred to the Archbishopric of York (which meant that he would find it difficult to attend future meetings of the Trustees held in London), and of Baron Hillingdon, whose continuing ill-health had prevented him from attending any of the meetings held so far. Mr Gillett then reported that he and Sir Walpole Greenwell had selected the Hon Arthur Brodrick and Colonel Sir Edward W. D. Ward to occupy two of the three places they were empowered to fill, and that they had another candidate in mind for the third place. The Trustees then resolved to appoint the new Bishop of Stepney, the Rt Revd H. L. Paget, as the first Additional Trustee to fill the vacancy created by the resignation

5. Colonel the Hon Arthur Grenville Brodrick.　　　6. Colonel Sir Edward Willis Duncan Ward.

of his predecessor. They also unanimously confirmed the Bishop of London as their Chairman.

The Trustees next heard a second report from the Executors about the realisation of the Estate, and were told that some progress had been made, including the satisfactory settlement of the action against them by the Executors of J. F. Benson & Co. In the light of the progress made, the Trustees again decided to leave the matter of further realisations to the discretion of the Executors for the time being. The Executors' report had also revealed that £65,000 was now available to be handed over to the Trustees, who decided to open an account for the Trust with the head office of the London & Westminster Bank, with the signatures of three Trustees being required to authorise the payment of a cheque. They then resolved to form a Finance Committee, to consist for the present of the whole body of Trustees, but with the presence of only three members being necessary to constitute a quorum. This Finance Committee was requested to consider the investment of the Trust's funds, and it was agreed that Messrs W. Greenwell & Co. should act as the Trust's brokers.

The Trustees were then informed that proceedings had been taken by the Executors to determine whether the legacy duty payable on the £1,000,000 bequeathed to the Trust should be paid out of that sum or out of the residue of the late Mr Whiteley's estate, and they decided to instruct solicitors to enter an appearance on their behalf and to retain counsel in order that proper arguments could be put to the court in favour of the duty being payable from the residue of the estate.

Discussion of a scheme for the establishment of the homes was again postponed as the Trustees were still not in a position to proceed with any such scheme, and it was clear that they would not be for some time to come.

The Trustees met for the fourth time on 13 July 1909. Present for the first time were the Hon Arthur Brodrick, Sir Edward Ward and Sir Edward F. Coates, MP, the third member appointed by Sir Walpole Greenwell and Mr Gillett, together with the new Bishop of Stepney. Mr Gillett reported that Mr Justice Eve, who had heard the case, had decided that the legacy duty was payable out of the residue of the estate and not out of the bequest itself. Additionally, the Trustees were entitled, also from the residue, as from one year after Mr Whiteley's death, to interest at the rate of four per cent per annum on so much of the amount due to them as remained unpaid up to the date on which it was paid. He added that William and Frank Whiteley had given notice of their intention to appeal against this ruling. The Whiteley brothers then withdrew from the meeting, and in their absence the remaining Trustees decided that the Trust's position ought to be maintained, and should be properly represented in court when the appeal was heard.

At this meeting, the Trustees also received a third report from the Executors, to whom they gave their formal receipt for £350,000, the total so far paid to them. The report told them that they could expect a further payment in the autumn of about £500,000.

The question of whether the homes should be concentrated or split up was then discussed, but only briefly. It was decided to make enquiries of other similar organisations to profit from their experiences. Some applications from architects offering their services and submissions from various agents regarding sites available for the homes were produced and, in view of these and of the work involved in supervising the assets now accruing to the Trust, the Trustees turned their attention to the need for a Trust Secretary to look after the Trust's affairs. A salary of £700 a year was agreed upon, and it was decided to make private enquiries in the first instance for '... a Gentleman who would be good at organisation and assisting the Trustees to formulate their Scheme ... rather than a man with powers of management such as might be required in such an Official at a later stage'. The Trustees considered that the appointment of a secretary had now become a matter of urgency, and agreed to meet again at an early date to consider the matter further.

They actually did so on 21 July 1909, but failed to reach any agreement. What they did do at this meeting, however, was to decide to approach a Mr Eyre (a candidate for the post of Secretary) and Mr Walter Cave, an architect, '... to ask them to separately formulate suggestions for the establishment of Homes, each of them to be offered 100 Guineas for his service and Report'. It was, however, to be made clear to Mr Eyre that this did not '... imply any determination of the Trustees to appoint him

Secretary and in the case of Mr Walter Cave that it was in no sense to imply that he would be employed as Architect'.

At their sixth meeting on 13 October 1909, the Trustees were told that a further £450,000 had been received from the Executors, making a total of £800,000 to date, and it was decided to transfer the Trust's bank account to the Amalgamated Bank of the London County & Westminster Ltd.

The Trustees then went on to consider the reports submitted by Mr Eyre and Mr Cave. Both of these recommended dividing the homes among a number of locations, Eyre suggesting as many as nine to twelve, and Cave suggesting four. A separate report, which had been prepared on the private instructions of Frank Whiteley, was also considered, and during the long discussion on this topic which then took place, both the Whiteley brothers strongly urged the desirability of placing the whole of the homes upon a single site to accommodate up to 800 persons, explaining that they felt sure this was what their late father had really intended. They again raised the question of the suitability for this purpose of the property at Hanworth, which was now owned by William Whiteley Ltd., and which the Chairman had visited. It was decided that, before coming to any decision, the other Trustees should also arrange to visit the site to see for themselves what was being proposed.

With regard to the appointment of a Secretary, a short-list of four candidates from those who had been put forward was agreed upon for consideration at the next meeting, which they were invited to attend for interview. This took place only 10 days later on 23 October 1909, when it was reported that another £40,000 had been received from the Executors. Mr Gillett then reported that the Court of Appeal had rejected the appeal by the Whiteley brothers against the earlier decision regarding the payment of legacy duty and interest payable on the outstanding amount, and in so doing had upheld Mr Justice Eve's judgement, which therefore stood.

The Trustees then turned their attention to the appointment of a secretary. Mr Eyre, one of the four who had been short-listed, had withdrawn his candidature, but the other three were each interviewed, and one of them, Mr Ingram, was appointed at the agreed salary of £700 a year subject to an annual deduction of £200 which was to be

> ... invested at compound interest for his benefit, this amount to be retained by the Trustees for the whole period, or for so long as they thought right, during the time of his service as Secretary, but to be Mr Ingram's property and to be handed over to him, with accumulations, on his ceasing to be their Secretary.

The Trustees then went on to consider the need for office accommodation. It was agreed that, for convenience, this should be located in the City, and a sub-committee consisting of Sir Walpole Greenwell, the Hon Arthur Brodrick and Major Coates was formed to acquire suitable premises within a maximum rent of £350 a year and on terms which would not commit the Trust to a tenancy exceeding three years.

The eighth meeting of the Trustees was held on 8 November 1909 and was a crucial one. Mr Ingram was in attendance, although he had not yet taken up his duties as Secretary. The main item on the agenda was the formulation of a scheme for the homes. A long discussion on this took place, and, as before, it became apparent that the majority of Trustees favoured the division of the homes among a number of sites, whereas both William and Frank Whiteley were strongly opposed to this plan and favoured a single site. They added that '... they felt bound to maintain this view because they believed it to be the real intention of the Testator'. After more discussion, it was agreed to seek counsel's opinion on this point with a view to obtaining the court's ruling, and, for their part, the Whiteley brothers agreed to accept the decision of the court and to co-operate with the other Trustees whichever way the matter was decided by the court. Another meeting was held shortly afterwards on 26 November, at which Mr Gillett produced the formal opinion of Mr Younger KC, who had been consulted, and which was to the effect that the Trustees had the discretion to found the homes on several sites if they so wished. However, despite this legal opinion, and the fact that all the other Trustees were in favour of a number of sites, the Whiteley brothers refused to give way, and it was accordingly agreed to take the matter to court. At the same time it was agreed that a ruling should be sought as to whether a majority of Trustees had the power to bind a dissenting minority. The case was heard by Mr Justice Eve on Wednesday, 23 February 1910, and decided in favour of the Whiteley brothers. (A full transcript of Mr Justice Eve's judgement is given in Appendix C.)

The Trustees met again a few days later on 28 February 1910, which was as soon as could be arranged after Mr Justice Eve's judgement, and immediately began to discuss how to proceed in view of his ruling. They now had to select a single suitable site, and to undertake this task they formed a Site Committee consisting of Sir Walpole Greenwell, Mr Frank Whiteley, the Hon Arthur Brodrick, Sir Edward Ward, and Sir Edward Coates. The instructions to this committee were '... to make a selection of suitable sites after taking into consideration such circumstances as the size of the houses required for the purposes of the Homes and the allowances to be made to prospective inmates, and to report to the Trustees'. No size for the site was defined, but 200 acres was suggested; the desirability of providing sufficient 'elbow room' was to be borne in mind, as was the possibility of part of the land being devoted to a recreation ground to be made available on occasion for games and sports to persons and parties other than inmates.

Having regard to more mundane matters the Trustees approved the acquisition of office premises at 4 London Wall Buildings at the previously stipulated rental on a seven-year lease determinable after three years, and agreed to spend £750 for fittings and furniture. They also approved the appointment of Mr C. H. Crawley as Assistant Secretary and book-keeper from 6 March at a salary of £200 a year, and of William Strudwick as office boy at a salary of 10s. per week. They also agreed to a refund of the travelling expenses incurred by the Secretary in connection with visits he had made on Trust business, and resolved that he should in future be permitted first-class travel. It was also agreed to leave it to his discretion when to take casual leave.

The Trustees next turned their attention to financial matters. The Secretary produced for them 'Financial Statement No. 1' which was approved. (This is reproduced in full in Appendix D.) They then empowered the Finance Committee to invest up to £250,000 of the Trust's assets and to renew the deposit arrangements in respect of the remainder. The signature of the Secretary was added to that of the three Trustees required for the authorisation of cheques. Approval was also given to the appropriation of securities by the Trust from the Executors to the agreed value of £62,693 16s. 3d. towards the payment of the legacy. It was also decided to replace the present Finance Committee consisting of the whole body of Trustees with a quorum of three by a new Finance Committee consisting of Lord Sandhurst, Sir Walpole Greenwell, Mr William Whiteley, the Hon Arthur Brodrick and Sir Edward Coates.

Things were at last really beginning to take shape. The new Sites Committee met for the first time a few days later on 7 March 1910, when Sir Edward Ward was voted into the chair, and met again on 16 March and 13 April. These meetings were the first to be held in the new Trust offices in London Wall Buildings. The committee agreed that a site of between 200 and 300 acres was required, and in the first instance they tried to keep their enquiries secret by using Mr Crawley, the Assistant Secretary, to make them on their behalf. As a result of his activities, sites at Hillingdon and Osterley were put forward for consideration together with two others at Crawley; one at Shirley Park and the other at Addington.

A period of intense activity now followed. The Trustees met on 4 May and again on 11 May, mainly to consider reports from the Sites Committee, but they failed to reach a decision. As a result of further enquiries, more sites were added to the list, and the Sites Committee met again on 1 June and 15 June followed by another meeting of the Trustees on 22 June, when they again failed to reach a decision. A further meeting of the Committee and the Trustees during July also failed to resolve the matter. A short lull followed to give the Trustees time to visit the sites which were then still under consideration. When the Sites Committee met again on 26 October 1910, they decided, Mr Frank Whiteley dissenting, that the Hanworth Farm site was not suitable, and that they should recommend the acquisition of the Shirley Park Estate at Croydon. At a meeting held later that same afternoon the Trustees accepted this recommendation by a majority with William and Frank Whiteley still dissenting. The Sites Committee and the Trustees each met again on 16 November and 7 December respectively, when the arguments for and against the purchase of the Shirley Park Estate were exhaustively discussed and again approved by a majority against the continued opposition of the Whiteley brothers. However, the purchase of land required the approval of the court, and when this was sought, the Whiteley brothers opposed the application on the grounds that Croydon was not situated in the 'Western Suburbs' of London, which was where their father, in Clause 31 of his will, had directed that the chosen site should be. The application was heard by Mr Justice Eve on 15 February 1911. In his judgement he said that he could not treat Croydon as a 'Western Suburb' and accordingly refused to sanction the purchase of the Shirley Park Estate by the Trustees. (A full transcript of Mr Justice Eve's judgement is given at Appendix E.)

After this second upset to their plans the Trustees met again as soon as they could on 24 February 1911 to decide how to proceed, and quickly resolved to adopt the definition of what constituted a Western Suburb contained in Mr Justice Eve's judgement. The Sites Committee was reactivated, and met on 17 March when five new sites were considered: Bentley Priory, Stanmore; a site at Ruislip; the Burhill Estate, outside Weybridge; the Odaford Park Estate, Iver; and Sayes Court, Addlestone.

The Trustees met shortly afterwards on 22 March and resolved unanimously that the Burhill Estate was the most suitable. A detailed survey was commissioned. This proved satisfactory, and when the Trustees next met on 7 April it was at Burhill, where they inspected the site. As a result of this inspection they agreed unanimously to proceed with the purchase '... for the whole 225 acres at the best price obtainable not exceeding £200 per acre'. When they next met in London on 3 May they were told that an offer of £40,000 for the whole 225 acres had been accepted subject to the sanction of the court, which, it was correctly anticipated, would now be readily forthcoming, as the site fell within Mr Justice Eve's definition of a 'Western Suburb'. Also the Trustees themselves were unanimous, which meant that the application would be unopposed.

It was now more than four years since Mr Whiteley's death, and this long delay had not gone unnoticed. A number of letters had been published in the press asking what had happened to his legacy. The Trustees, however, were now ready to proceed. They had received the full legacy from the executors, and had found a suitable site. Their next task was to develop that site in order to provide homes for the aged poor.

Chapter Three

PLANNING A VILLAGE FOR THE ELDERLY (1911-14)

The vendors now discovered that they had mislaid one of the principal title deeds to the Burhill Estate. Without this deed the sale of the estate to the Whiteley Homes Trust could not proceed, and when it became apparent that the deed really had been lost, there was considerable consternation! The problem was overcome by the execution of a 'Deed of Confirmation of lost Deed of conveyance of 1st December 1880' – that being the date on which that part of the estate to which the lost deed related had last changed hands. The need to execute this new deed caused a good deal of delay, which meant that, although the Trustees had unanimously agreed on 7 April 1911 to go ahead with the purchase of the estate, it was not until late June that they were able to proceed in the matter, and not until 18 July that they were able to obtain the sanction of the court (again given by Mr Justice Eve) to make the purchase.

Meanwhile, the Trustees were not idle. Despite the temporary inability of their Chairman to attend meetings because of his heavy involvement as Lord Bishop of London in the preparations for the Coronation of King George V, who had succeeded to the throne the previous year, they met three times during May and twice in June. At these meetings they principally concerned themselves with matters relating to the Burhill Estate, which indicates that, despite the uncertainty which must have been occasioned by the lost deed, they felt confident that they would ultimately be able to proceed with its purchase.

Firstly, they were concerned to ensure that adequate drainage for the buildings to be erected on the site would be available, and Mr J. H. Oakley (of Messrs D. Smith Son & Oakley, a firm of surveyors who had helped the Trustees find the site) was commissioned to investigate the position with Walton Urban District Council on their behalf. Mr (later Sir John) Oakley, who was to become increasingly involved on behalf of the Trustees in matters connected with the estate, subsequently reported to the Trustees that he had received satisfactory assurances from the council on this matter, which were accepted. Secondly, the Trustees decided to have an accurate survey made of the site, and this was also entrusted to Messrs D. Smith Son & Oakley.

In addition, it had become clear that the house known as 'Fox Oak' (which was situated on the western boundary of the estate adjoining the Seven Hills Road) was for sale, and Mr Oakley was instructed to negotiate the purchase of this property within a limit of £5,000. This offer was declined, but later in the year the Trustees increased their offer for it to £7,000, which was accepted. However, it was not until early in 1912 that the sanction of the court was obtained for the purchase of this property, which then became part of the estate.

At this stage, the Trustees from time to time had considerable discussions about the form which the homes should take without coming to any formal agreement on the subject, but a general consensus of opinion amongst them had nevertheless emerged regarding the following points:

> That 500 should be the maximum number of inmates for whom provision should be made.

> That 7s. 6d. (37½p) '... in cash should constitute a weekly allowance to be given to each person whether married or single and be in addition to such benefits, comforts, privileges, and amenities as the Trustees might decide should be shared by all'.

> That applicants should be chosen regardless of whether or not they were entitled to an Old Age Pension (which very few were at that time).

It should be remembered that, in 1911, the Trustees had no precedent to guide them as to the form the homes should take, or as to the amenities to be provided, because this was the first project of its kind in this country on such a large scale. They were truly innovators in this field, and it is therefore not surprising that they took time to come to firm decisions on such important and fundamental matters, or that having apparently done so at a particular meeting they should nevertheless subsequently return to the matter and change their minds, as indeed they were to do, sometimes several times. What they really did decide at this stage was that, firstly, they would hold a competition for the planning of the site so as to generate ideas from the leading architects of the day for them to consider, and secondly, that whatever form they eventually decided the homes should take, they '... would need at their disposal the advice of an Architect to assist them in deciding on points arising in connection with the laying out of the Homes'.

They addressed themselves first to the appointment of a consulting architect and one of them, Sir Edward Ward, was deputed to approach Mr Walter Cave with a view to retaining his services in that capacity. However some potential conflict of interests quickly became apparent which centred around whether or not, if Mr Cave were to be appointed consulting architect to the Trust, he would be eligible to take part in the proposed competition for the planning of the homes. Mr Cave attended one of the Trustees' meetings, and after explaining to them the duties which would normally devolve upon a consulting architect, went on to indicate '... certain difficulties which might arise if the Consulting Architect competed or if The Trustees were to appoint an Architect to revise or supervise the work of another Architect whether appointed directly or as the result of competition'. As a result of further discussion at a later meeting it was

> Resolved that a Consulting Architect should be appointed for 3 years certain at a salary not exceeding £1,000 per annum on the understanding that the duties involved were to be purely advisory, that the Trustees' discretion as to the Architects to be employed for any planning or construction work was to be left entirely unfettered, and that the appointee was to be debarred from competing ...

It was then also resolved that Mr Walter Cave should be offered the appointment. After considerable further negotiation Mr Cave accepted the appointment on the terms set out in Appendix F.

Having secured Mr Cave's appointment as their adviser, the Trustees turned their attention, in consultation with him, to the terms of the competition they proposed to hold for the general layout of the site (which they called the 'block plan') and a 'Schedule of Preliminary Questions' was prepared for consideration (see Appendix G). On the basis of this schedule, it was decided that:

The competition should be limited, and that the names of the competitors should be supplied by Mr Cave.

Each competitor should be paid £50 for his plans (this sum also to cover his expenses) and that in addition there would be three prizes: first prize – £150; second prize – £100; third prize – £50.

Each competitor would be provided with a copy of the survey plan.

The homes should mainly be of one storey with a few two-storeyed cottages. (It is worthy of note that this was the first time the term 'cottage' was used in connection with the Trust.)

The numbers to be accommodated should be initially based on 500 (as previously agreed) but leaving room for a possible expansion to 800.

Competitors should be told that there was a possibility of the property known as 'Fox Oak' being purchased and included in the estate. (It should, however, be noted that the estate did not, at that time, include the area in the north-west corner of the site which is bounded by the Seven Hills Road and the Burwood Road which is now called 'High Park'.)

The Trustees themselves would be the assessors, assisted only by their consulting architect. Consideration was given to the inclusion of a forestry expert, but this was decided against.

At this time it was also decided:

That as the nearest Anglican church was over a mile away in Hersham, provision should be made for a church on the site.

That a cemetery should be provided, it being felt that '... the prospect of honourable interment would be an inducement to old people ...' to live in the village.

That an infirmary should be provided.

That a bakehouse '... was to be regarded as a doubtful necessity'.

'Not to make provision for a Gas Station or Fire Engine Station.'

That there should be 'Allotment Gardens'.

Mr Cave was then instructed, at a meeting held on 26 July 1911, to draw up the necessary regulations for a competition reflecting these decisions. Unfortunately, these regulations were not preserved amongst the Trust records, and so cannot be reproduced here.

During this period, the Trustees also turned their attention to a number of other matters connected with the estate. The question of its protection was given early consideration, and it was decided to fence it, the Secretary being requested to obtain details of the various types of fencing available, and their cost. In addition, the surveyors were asked to make arrangements with the existing keeper to continue to look after it, and for him to be '... especially vigilant ...' with regard to trespassers. On the other hand, it was decided not to effect an insurance policy at this juncture. It was also decided, on Mr Oakley's advice, that the grazing tenancy of a Mr Isaac M. Hodgkinson and the shooting tenancy of a Mr McCaul should be allowed to continue for the present, and that Burhill Golf Club should also be allowed to continue their use of a 2½-acre paddock and five poultry houses subject to three months' notice being given when the Trustees wanted to end this arrangement. At that time, too, the pond was very choked, and Mr Oakley was instructed to have it cleared.

Mr Crawley, the Trust's Assistant Secretary and book-keeper, resigned his post early in 1911, and Mr C. M. Hennell, who was a qualified surveyor, was appointed in his place in May of that year. Shortly after taking up his appointment, Mr Hennell moved into rented accommodation in Walton so that he would be readily on hand to supervise the increasing activity which was taking place on the estate. However, when the Trust obtained vacant possession of Fox Oak on 15 May 1912, it was decided to make available to him a flat within the house, and

> ... that Mr Hennells [sic] should be repaid the wages of two domestic servants to be engaged and paid by him – estimated to amount to rather more than £40 per annum – and that he should be allowed fuel and light, also vegetables from the kitchen garden, he keeping account of the quantity consumed, the surplus to be sold.

In addition, a Mr Edwards and a Mr Mills, who had been employed by the previous owners of Fox Oak as their gardener and under-gardener respectively, were taken on by the Trust in the same capacities. Edwards was employed

> ... at 24/-[£1.20] per week on the understanding that he should be prepared to live in the house or stables and that if the Trustees required the services of his wife as well as of himself (including any simple cooking as might from time-to-time be required) they would be prepared to pay him at a higher rate but not exceeding 35/-[£1.75] per week.

That part of the house not being occupied by Hennell was furnished and equipped for use by the Trustees when visiting the estate, and a telephone was installed. A proposal to purchase a motor-car for their use on such occasions was, however, postponed for later consideration.

The estate was at that time quite heavily wooded, and, although the Trustees had decided not to involve a forestry expert in the assessment of the plans for the layout of the village, they nevertheless felt they needed advice on this subject and accordingly appointed a Mr Bartlett, '... an expert recommended by the Kew Garden authorities ...', at a fee of 2 guineas (£2.10) per day plus third-class travelling expenses to prepare a report for them on what needed doing. The preparation of this report, which is unfortunately not to be found amongst the Trust records, occupied Bartlett for three days, as a result of which he was engaged '... to carry out some of his recommendations ...' on the following terms:

(1)   That he was to be remunerated at the rate of 3 Guineas [£3.15] per week, this remuneration to cover all superintendence, reports, and work to be done by him;

(2)   That he was to be responsible for the superintendence of the work generally, and for its being properly carried out;

7.   Fox Oak.

(3) That he was to be responsible for the foreman-woodman and labourers employed, who were to be paid and engaged by him – the foreman-woodman to receive not more than 32/6d [£1.62½p] per week (to include board and lodging) and the labourers not more than 6d [2½p] per hour;

(4) The work to be done was that connected with the Lime Avenue [which then ran right across the estate from the point on the Seven Hills Road where the West Gate is now situated to the eastern boundary] viz: the removal of fallen or dead trees and injurious insects as referred to in his Report;

(5) All necessary plant (tools, ladders, etc.) were to be purchased by him but were to be approved before purchase both as to quality and price by Mr Oakley and the Secretary. All plant to be marked 'WT'.

Mr Bartlett set to work with a will, but Mr Cave, on visiting the estate early in 1912, was horrified at what he was doing, and took it upon himself to order him to stop at once. This action was ratified by the Trustees who quickly came to see for themselves what had been going on, and fresh instructions were issued to Bartlett who, it was agreed, had genuinely misunderstood what he was required to do.

At a meeting held on 4 October 1911, Mr Cave put forward the names of the following architects who he suggested might be invited to take part in the competition:

Sir Aston Webb, RA, CB
Mr Reginald T. Blomfield, ARA
Mr John Belcher, RA
Mr Henry T. Hare*
Mr C. L. Lutyens
Mr R. Frank Atkinson*
Mr Ernest Newton, ARA
Mr Thomas B. Colcutt*
Mr Mervyn E. Macartney*
Messrs Parker and Unwin
Mr J. W. Paul

The Trustees deputed Mr Cave to invite six of these to compete, with the proviso that '... in the event of less than six deciding to compete he should nominate others for selection by the Trustees'. In the event, all but the four of those on the list above whose names are marked with an asterisk declined the invitation, and so a second list was submitted by Mr Cave and approved by the Trustees on 28 February 1912, as follows:

Sir Ernest George, ARA*
Professor Stanley Davenport Adshead, FRIBA*
Mr H. Inigo Triggs, FRIBA

Mr Geoffrey Lucas, FRIBA
Mr E. Guy Dauber, FRIBA
Mr Sidney K. Greenslade, ARIBA

Of those on the second list, again only the two whose names are marked with an asterisk accepted the invitation, but this made the total of competitors up to six, which was the minimum number the Trustees wanted. The date by which the competitors were to be required to submit their plans was set at 1 May, which gave them a bare two months to prepare them!

Towards the end of 1911, a sub-committee of the Trustees appointed for the purpose met at Burhill to select the fencing for the estate. English oak fencing 5 ft. 9 in. in height with nails on the capping had been specified, and the following tenders were received:

Messrs William Stenning & Son:	£1,944 0s. 0d.
Mr E. C. White:	£1,963 15s. 0d.
The Economic Fencing Co:	£1,974 7s. 6d.
Messrs B. Horton & Son:	£2,067 15s. 0d.

The sub-committee, having inspected specimens of the fencing produced by each of the firms, recommended that the contract should be awarded to Messrs William Stenning & Son. At first, it was intended that oak fencing of the type specified should be erected around the whole perimeter of the estate, but in order '... to give the Trustees and inmates a better view of the surrounding country on that side than would be afforded them by a close fence ...', it was decided to modify the original plan and use open iron fencing along the eastern boundary. The contract was modified accordingly, which resulted in some compensation having to be paid to Messrs William Stenning & Son.

By 1 May 1912 only five of the six competitors had submitted their plans. The plans themselves had been opened by Sir Walpole Greenwell and Sir Edward Coates on 2 May, but the sealed envelopes containing the name of each competitor and identifying his plans had been deposited unopened in the Trust safe. At a meeting held on 8 May it was decided that formal consideration of the plans would take place on 18 May, which would allow time for Mr Cave and Mr Oakley to prepare a report on the plans to assist the Trustees when they came to judge them. Then, on 10 May, the sixth and final set of plans was received. An emergency meeting was held on 13 May to decide what to do, and, after considerable discussion, it was

Resolved that the Secretary shall open the parcel containing the plans and the sealed envelope containing the Competitor's name but that he should not disclose the latter to any of the Trustees or to Mr Cave or to Mr Oakley and that he should write to the Competitor and inform him that his plans arrived out of time but that they had not been seen and would not be seen by the Trustees or by Mr Cave or by Mr Oakley pending his reply, and further that the Trustees could not in the circumstances consider his plans for the purposes of the prizes offered but that they would be prepared to pay him £50 as a recompense for his trouble and the additional £50 provided for by the Conditions for the Competition if they decided to utilise them, and that if he was not prepared to agree to these terms that the Secretary's instructions were to return the plans to him unseen.

The competitor concerned obviously did agree to those conditions because when the Trustees met at Fox Oak on 18 May to judge the plans, all six sets were considered. For identification they had been labelled simply 'U', 'V', 'W', 'X', 'Y' and 'Z' and, having read the joint report prepared for them by Mr Cave and Mr Oakley, the Trustees decided to award the first prize to plan 'W', the second prize to plan 'X', and the third prize to plan 'Z'. On opening the sealed envelopes it was found that the winner was Mr R. Frank Atkinson, and that Mr Thomas B. Colcutt and Professor Adshead had won the second and third prizes respectively. Plan 'U' (which was the one which had arrived late) was that submitted by Mr Henry T. Hare; that marked 'V' was that of Mr Mervyn E. Macartney; that marked 'Y' was that of Sir Ernest George. These plans, with the exception of plan 'Y' which is missing from the Trust's records, are reproduced in alphabetical order at Appendix H. Having made their decision the Trustees wasted no time, and before adjourning their meeting

... decided to proceed with making roads and sewers as soon as possible, and, as a preliminary step the Consulting Architect and Mr Oakley were instructed to reconsider the winning designs and, using Mr Atkinson's design as a basis, to confer and report to the Trustees as to the best means of giving effect to his scheme, as modified by the suggestions made by the Consulting Architect and Mr Oakley in their Joint Report ...

The Secretary was also instructed to announce the result of the competition in the press. Finally, at the end of what must have been a very busy day, the Trustees decided that the official designation of the charity should be 'The Whiteley Homes' and that the estate should in future be known as 'Whiteley Park'.

At the end of February 1912, Lord Sandhurst indicated that he wished to resign his Trusteeship, and, despite being requested by the other Trustees to reconsider his decision on the understanding that he would not in future be expected to give the Trust so much of his time as before, he declined to change his mind. Sir Arthur Griffith-Boscawen MP was appointed in his place.

Being a Trustee of The Whiteley Homes had at that time become a genuinely onerous task. The Trustees held eight meetings during the second half of 1911, and a further eight by mid-May 1912 when they judged the competition for the block plan, and there were very few of those meetings which were not attended by every one of them. This increase in the volume of Trust business also meant that the Secretary was often finding it difficult to get a sufficiently quick response on urgent matters which needed to be decided by the Trustees because he could only refer it to them at one of their meetings. So, in order both to speed up the decision-making process and to try to reduce the work-load for the majority of Trustees, an Executive

Committee was formed, consisting of Sir Walpole Greenwell, the Hon Arthur Brodrick, and Sir Edward Coates, '... to whom the Secretary could refer in emergency on all matters on which he found he needed interim instructions. It was resolved that this Committee should have power to act in matters which in their discretion were sufficiently urgent to justify action pending reference to a Meeting of the Trustees'. There is very little evidence, however, that this arrangement actually worked in practice, and throughout this period the Trust records show that almost every decision of any importance at all was taken at a meeting of the full body of Trustees, and that they met frequently in order to cope with this workload. In addition, there was certainly no question at this stage of delegating any real powers of decision-making to their Secretary, Mr Ingram, who, it will be remembered, had been appointed for his organisational rather than for his management skills.

8. R. Frank Atkinson.

The revisions to Frank Atkinson's prize-winning plan proposed by Mr Cave and Mr Oakley and accepted by the Trustees were substantial, as can be seen by comparing the copy of his plan (W) in Appendix H with the map of the village dated September 1919 in Appendix K, which has been amended to include all the buildings completed up to June 1922. This comparison reveals that almost the only feature of any significance in Mr Atkinson's plan which was retained was his concept of an octagonal layout for the central portion of the village, and that most of the rest was discarded. No reasons are given in the Trust records for such a radical curtailment of the plan, but it seems likely that it was made on the basis of the Trustees' decision that the maximum number of inmates to be accommodated should initially be limited to 500. However, as will become apparent, if the decision had not been made then a reduction of similar size would have been forced upon the Trustees later by building costs.

Before any building work of any sort could be started, it was necessary to clear the trees and scrub covering the area to be built over. At a meeting held in mid-June 1912, the Trustees

Resolved that as a preliminary step before finally deciding the width of the main road an opening for the main road should be cut along its length from the point in Burwood Road marked in Mr Cave's plan through the main (lime) avenue to the points where it was proposed in Mr Cave's plan to end the Cottages, and that this cutting should be 20 ft. wide ...

The cutting would have run from the North Lodge at the entrance gate on to the Burwood Road to the point where South Avenue joins Octagon Road (see map, Appendix K). Mr Oakley, who had by now been appointed the Trust's consulting surveyor, was instructed that, although the tops of the felled trees could be kept and used for firewood, the remainder were to be sold when a favourable opportunity offered. As building work progressed, further clearings had to be made, especially in the area around and within the perimeter of the Octagon. From the first, however, the Trustees gave strict instructions that, so far as was possible, the good trees were to be preserved, and the character of the completed village was undoubtedly much enhanced by that decision.

At the same meeting in mid-June 1912 the Trustees also asked Mr Cave to prepare a complete set of plans for a 'Model Cottage' to be built under his directions so that

9. The Lime Avenue (East).

10. Clearings for the main road.

they '... might see the internal accommodation and elevation which he would propose that the Cottages should have'. They also decided to appoint two clerks of works: one to oversee the building of the roads and sewers and the other to oversee the construction of the buildings. Mr Thomas Mitchell was appointed to the former post in October of that year, and Mr Frank Comport to the latter post in May 1913. As regards the provision of water, power, and light, the Trustees decided that they needed expert advice, and Mr Cave was '... authorised to engage the services of Mr H. D. Wilkinson and Mr W. Vaux Graham at a remuneration not exceeding forty Guineas [£42] to cover both fees'.

As already mentioned, the Trustees were anxious to proceed as quickly as possible with the construction of the roads and sewers as the obvious first step in the building of the village. They accordingly wasted no time in deciding what they wanted, which was:

To have greenswards next to the roads, with paths beyond the greenswards. The width of the greenswards was originally fixed at 6 ft. 6 in., but this was later increased to 13 ft.

For there to be curbing between the metalling of the roads and the greenswards.

That in places '... where the contour of the roads necessitated an embankment or cuttings, the greensward to slope to the path and the path [to] lie on a lower or a higher level as the case might be rather than the path to be on the same level as the road and the slope of the embankment start from the outside edge of the path' [sic].

That '... the main road (from north to south) exclusive of the roadway to the Bridge, to rise in a gradual slope from the North Entrance to the central point of the Estate so as to give an uninterrupted view of the Memorial [which it was proposed to erect there] and south of that point gradually to follow the contour of the land so far as was practicable bearing in mind that where it crossed the Octagon Road the surface level of both roads must be 3 ft below the ground level' [sic].

That '... the curbing of this road to be of granite, splayed and 2 ins wide at the top with rounded nose'.

That '... the corners at the junctions of the road with Octagon Road to be rounded off with curves of a radius of 6 ft'.

That '... the curbing of the subsidiary roads [should be] smaller, as small as consistent with [adequate] strength'.

That '... the paths [should not be] perfectly straight, but to wind in and out of the trees and other obstructions' [sic].

That '... the construction of the Bridge [should be] considered later, mean-while a temporary piece of roadway to be taken round the edge of the lake'.

The Trustees also decided that

> ... the roads and sewers should be under their control (notwithstanding the consideration that if the roads were thrown open to the public The Trustees would get some return for the rates they would have to pay) and that conse-quently no claim of the local authorities to interfere in the construction of the roads should be entertained.

Despite this initial attempt at independence, in practice they soon found that it was necessary for them to obtain the agreement of the local council to their proposals in order to ensure that no statutory requirements or local by-laws were infringed. In fact, the negotiations with the local council proved to be somewhat protracted, and agreement with them was not finally reached until the middle of 1913. Meanwhile, in January of that year Mr Oakley had sent out the schedule, specification and plans for the roads to a selection of contractors inviting them to tender. The specification called for a 9-in. deep base of hardcore topped by 6 in. of gravel metalling. In April the tenders were considered by the Trustees, and the contract was awarded to Messrs Hiram Moorcroft & Co.

With regard to the water supply for the village, Mr Vaux Graham, having had an analysis of the water in the pond carried out by Messrs Allen & Hanbury Ltd., recom-mended to the Trustees that they should accept the offer of the West Surrey Water Company to supply water to the village at a special flat rate of 8d. per 1,000 gallons, provided that all the water required on the estate was taken from them. This was agreed.

With regard to the supply of gas and electricity, however, the Trustees were of two minds, and asked Mr Wilkinson

> ... to advise in conjunction with the Consulting Architect and Consulting Surveyor:

> (a) As to the relative cost of gas and electricity for all or any of the purposes for which supply was needed, such as road and house lighting, cooking and heating, power, and any other purposes.

> (b) As to The Trustees making their own gas or electricity and the cost thereof.

> (c) As to the connections that would have to be made if the supply was taken from outside.

> (d) As to the combination of gas and electric supply and the purposes for which each would be used, and

> (e) Generally.

When Mr Wilkinson presented his report, he advised the Trustees to use electricity rather than gas for cooking as well as for lighting, and recommended that if they did so they should generate their own supply, adding that if they decided to use electricity for lighting purposes only, they should use the local company's supply. In his report Mr Wilkinson also raised the question as to whether electricity should be used for heating, but '... the Trustees were of opinion that coal fires should not be dispensed with in the Cottages'.

At first, the Trustees accepted Mr Wilkinson's advice that they should generate their own supply of electricity, and went on to specify that: '... the lighting of the roads should be by incandescent electric light and that a special point should be made of providing pilot lamps to burn all night throughout the Estate at corners and dark places'. They also decided that

> ... the gas supply should be taken from the Gas Company so far as required for cooking purposes [thus rejecting Mr Wilkinson's advice that electricity should be used for that purpose] but that although mains for the gas should be laid ... at the present stage ... [they] ... should not commit themselves to the principle of providing gas stoves in all the Cottages in addition to open grates.

It is worthy of note that under the terms of the agreement entered into, the mains were laid and paid for by the Trust and not by the gas company, and that they therefore belonged to the Trust and not to the gas company. In later years, this was to be regretted when the pipes began to corrode.

Walter Cave wasted no time in drawing up his plans for what turned out to be a pair of 'Model Cottages' and these were presented to the Trustees and approved at a meeting held at Fox Oak on Monday, 22 July 1912. A contract for building them (for the sum of £1,383) was soon placed, and by the following February it was reported to the Trustees that they were almost finished, and at another meeting held at Fox Oak on Saturday, 19 April 1913 the Trustees were able to inspect the completed cottages. As a result of this inspection, the Trustees decided '... that the general type of Cottage to be erected should be smaller [and] that the joinery and other exposed woodwork should be of oak or other hardwood'. They also decided to pay an official visit to Hampstead Garden Suburb to see what was being done there in order to help them decide upon the standard of accommodation to be provided in the village. There is, however, no evidence that this visit influenced them in any particular way.

The question of the provision to be made for those who, at this stage, are constantly referred to in the Trust records as the 'inmates' of the village, was one that was ever-present in the Trustees' minds throughout this period, and one which they constantly discussed at their meetings. On 22 July 1912 they finally came to some definite conclusions, and, having confirmed their previous decision that applicants should be chosen regardless of whether or not they were entitled to an Old Age Pension, they formally resolved that:

> There should be uniformity of accommodation provided in the class of Cottage to be built, subject to any necessary modifications for single inmates or married couples, and to architectural differences.

11. The Model Cottages.

No rent should be charged and that the holding should be free of rates and taxes.

Instead of paying a standard weekly allowance of 7s. 6d. a week to all inmates (as they had previously agreed to do) they '... contemplated the payment to inmates of weekly allowances so that inmates should have at least 7/6d in cash'.

A small extra room suitable for guests should be provided in each of the Cottages but that it should be an understanding that this room was strictly under the control of the Charity.

The benefits to be shared by all should consist of: an annual allowance of coal; light; water; medical and nursing attendance.

The following benefits, comforts, and conveniences should be available to inmates at nominal charges and under conditions [which were not specified]: charwomen; gardeners; laundry; drying room; dairy produce; common bathroom; clubroom and library.

A bakehouse should not be provided and that the Charity should not undertake to provide garden produce.

The proportion of single and double cottages should be half-and-half.

Provision should not be made for common dining-rooms '... other than in connection with the Administration Block'.

Shop and market accommodation should be provided '... in connection with the administration block'.

(At this stage it seems likely that the Trustees were themselves not certain exactly what they had in mind when they referred to an 'Administration Block'. It is quite clear that they did not mean just an office, and that their main concern was the provision of facilities to cater for inmates who became temporarily or permanently incapable of looking after themselves or who needed to be isolated because they had contracted an infectious or contagious disease.)

12. Left to right: ?; ?; Sir Walpole Greenwell; Colonel Brodrick; Henry Luke Paget; Sir Ernest George; Bishop Winnington-Ingram; Sir Edward Coates; William Whiteley Jnr; William Gillett; ?; ?.

That there should be both a male and a female Superintendent [and] that the female should be unmarried and that both should be of a superior class.

That local offices should be provided in the Administration Block but that the Boardroom and Trustees' Rooms should be at 'Fox Oak'.

That in view of the fact that groups of the Homes would be disjointed [sic] each group should be placed in charge of some permanent member of the Staff who would be housed in the group, and that ... all groups should be connected by telephone with the central and nursing block.

The Trustees returned to the subject later that year when, at a meeting held on 11 November, they:

Reversed their earlier decision to provide a guest room in each cottage, and decided instead to consider the provision of a separate guest house.

Decided '... that each group of cottages should have attached to them for the common use of the residents a building containing a small laundry and drying room, wash-house for baths, and lavatory accommodation'.

Requested their consulting architect to draw up a plan for an 'administration block' based on the following requirements:

'That 30 "cottages of rest" should be provided for the accommodation of residents requiring special attention.'

'That 4 infirmary wards should be provided with 10 beds each, but capable of holding a maximum of 50 patients in all and that accommodation should be provided for attendants in connection therewith, namely: 1 matron; 1 house-keeper; 4 sisters; 15 nurses; 6 wardmaids; 1 cook and staff; housemaids; 1 porter and other male attendants.'

That (as a result of detailed enquiries as to the cost of running their own laundry, which included an examination of the arrangements at the Royal Hospital Chelsea) '... the general washing should be done by contract but that a small laundry should be provided in connection with the infirmary wards and that provision should be made therein for disinfecting clothes'.

'That staff reading, smoking, and dining rooms should be provided.'

'That a common dining room for inmates should be provided in connection with the administration portion of the block and probably another in connec-tion with the clubhouse or elsewhere on the site.'

That a garage should be built '... capable of accommodating motor omnibuses (for the use of the inmates) and several motor cars and that the yard should be roofed-in sufficiently to provide shelter for carts when being loaded or unloaded'.

'That workshops should be provided for the recreation of inmates but should be built some distance from the infirmary blocks.'

'That there should be a small strongroom or large safe.'

'Also a telephone exchange.'

'Also a heating chamber.'

'Also an office of works with administration workshops attached some distance from the infirmary wards.'

'That provison should be made for a covered-in central market ...'

'That provision should be made for an assistant superintendent and for a clerk or clerks.'

'That quarters for one engineer at least should be provided.'

'Also for a number of domestic servants.'

Consideration was also given to the appointment of a resident medical officer, it being suggested that perhaps a local practitioner '... might be induced to live in the homes and carry out his outside practice from there'. The question as to whether or not to build a separate house for a medical officer was deferred for later consideration, but as a temporary measure it was decided that '... two good rooms for a medical officer ...' should be included in the plan '... together with a dispensary'.

As early as mid-1912 Mr Cave had suggested to the Trustees that they should authorise him to select three or four architects to design separate blocks of cottages in conjunction with him so that they '... might get the advantage of variety without formal competition and at the same time obtain, for aesthetic and general purposes, a controlling influence ...'. At that time the Trustees agreed with his proposal, but early in 1913 decided that rather than let Mr Cave select the architects they would, after all, run a formal competition for the design of the central blocks of cottages within the Octagon. However, at a meeting held in early April of that year, they had second thoughts about the desirability of running a competition, and asked Mr Cave '... to discuss the whole question with Sir Aston Webb and Professor Reginald Blomfield and report their recommendations ...'.

At the next meeting of the Trustees, held a little later that month, Mr Cave reported that Sir Aston Webb and Professor Blomfield were of the opinion

... that a competition for the whole Village would not be practical, or one in which Architects of good standing would [wish to] compete; also that it would involve great loss of time; [and] that they recommended a division of the Village into Sections apportioned out to selected Architects, as such a course would lead to healthy rivalry and enable each Architect to be in full touch with each other and with The Trustees.

A long discussion followed, at the end of which the Trustees changed their minds yet again and decided to revert to Mr Cave's original suggestion,

... on the understanding that it would be possible to get at least four Architects of good standing ... to collaborate under the general supervision of the Consulting Architect as [their] representative in such a way that there might be complete intercommunication of design and The Trustees might have complete control and discretion at every stage.

It was then decided that the architects to be approached should be Sir Aston Webb, Professor Reginald Blomfield, Mr R. Frank Atkinson, Mr Mervyn Macartney, Mr Ernest Newton and Sir Ernest George, all of whom agreed to participate. The arrangement was that each 'opening' from Octagon Road to the centre of the village was allocated to an architect who was to be responsible for designing the cottages in half of the block of cottages on either side of that opening, the façades on each side of the opening to match each other. These blocks of cottages became known as 'sections' and they are still called this today. The allocation of 'openings' to architects was as follows, each being allocated one except Sir Ernest George who was given two, with Walter Cave, the Trust's own consulting architect, being allotted the eighth:

North Avenue:	Professor Reginald Blomfield
Hornbeam Walk:	Sir Ernest George
East Avenue:	Mr Ernest Newton
Heather Walk:	Sir Ernest George
South Avenue:	Mr Mervyn Macartney
The Green:	Sir Aston Webb
West Avenue:	Mr R. Frank Atkinson
Chestnut Walk:	Mr Walter Cave

On 12 June 1913, less than two months after they had decided that his 'Model Cottages' were too large (and therefore too expensive), Mr Cave produced to the Trustees a number of new sketch plans for cottages, from which they selected two which they considered best represented their revised view as to the level of accommodation to be provided. Mr Cave was then instructed to provide copies of these sketch plans to the participating architects to '... indicate The Trustees' wishes as to accommodation'. These sketch plans were shortly afterwards supplemented by some more precise details as to what the Trustees now required which they had agreed at a meeting held on 8 July, as follows:

That each of the 8 Sections of the Octagon should contain 16 single cottages with one floor for 16 single pensioners [sic]; 4 cottages with two floors for 8 single pensioners (one pensioner on each floor); 6 double cottages (1 couple in each) for 12 pensioners in couples, making a total of 26 cottages for 36 pensioners in each section; also 1 nurses' cottage or cottage in which could reside a nurse or other female competent to look after the pensioners in the section;

The accommodation in the pensioners' cottages to be one living room with an alcove bed recess, a scullery with lavatory basin and a sink of sufficient size to enable small articles to be washed in it, a larder, a coal store to take 2 sacks of coal, and a WC; coppers for washing not to be provided.

The nurses' cottages to consist of sitting room, bedroom, kitchen and bathroom and WC, also 2 spare bedrooms and 1 bathroom for pensioners, the last mentioned bathroom to be on the ground floor.

The dimensions for the rooms of the double cottages for pensioners to be greater than those of the single cottages. It was felt that in the double cottages the alcove for the bed should be of sufficient size to allow at least one of the pensioners to dress there without going into the living room, but that it was desirable further to consider the matter.

To help the Trustees come to a firm conclusion on this matter, the Whiteley brothers offered to build a mock-up of a cottage in rough materials with rooms of the proposed dimensions at their company's premises and to furnish these, so that the Trustees could see for themselves how much moving space the proposed dimensions would afford. As a result of inspecting this dummy cottage, several modifications were agreed upon, and fresh plans drawn up. A sketch illustrating this agreed level of 'Standard Accommodation' is reproduced in Appendix J.

Each of the architects was then asked to nominate a builder to be invited to tender for the contract for building the eight sections of cottages within the Octagon, it being the Trustees' initial intention that each of the builders approached should submit a tender for one of the groups and for the whole eight groups. Later, they changed their minds, and decided that it would be better to employ a single builder for the whole of the work, and the seven builders who had been nominated were invited to tender on that basis.

Their tenders were opened on Thursday, 2 April 1914, and were as follows:

Messrs Benfield & Loxley:	£134,668
J. Carmichael:	£126,964
Messrs Foster & Dicksee:	£131,163
Messrs Holland, Hannen & Cubitt:	£127,777
Holloway Bros:	£126,875
Henry Martin:	£116,968
Messrs Trollope & Colls.:	£137,065

The lowest tender, that of Henry Martin Ltd., was, however, considerably in excess of the amount the Trustees had allocated for this work in their budget. This took account of the need for enough of the initial bequest to be left unspent after the building of the village had been completed to provide, when it had been invested, an income that would be sufficient not only to maintain the village and pay the staff that would be required to run it, but also to give the inmates the weekly allowances that had been agreed upon. They decided, therefore, not to accept any of the tenders as they stood, but directed Mr Cave to enter into negotiation with Henry Martin Ltd. to see if they could reduce their price.

When the Trustees met again about a month later, Mr Cave told them that Henry Martin Ltd. were unable to reduce their prices in any way unless the specifications were modified. He then went on to tell them that, this being so, he had held a meeting with the other architects to discuss what modifications to the original specification might sensibly be made to reduce the cost, and produced a tabulated statement showing the cost of the original specification and five suggested reductions in columns labelled 'A' to 'F'. This statement is reproduced in Appendix K, the difference between the total cost shown in column 'A' of the statement and Henry Martin's tender as quoted above being accounted for by provisions for building a sleeper road round the lake to enable the contractors to get materials on to the site, for building a memorial and holding an opening ceremony. The Trustees decided to adopt alternative 'C', and the contract was placed with Henry Martin Ltd. on that basis.

In addition to the cottages to be built within the Octagon, there were several other buildings which the Trustees had decided should be provided, for example:

At the two main entrances, gates and two lodges, one on each side, and at the back entrance (by which they meant the entrance from Chestnut Avenue) a gate and a lodge on one side only ... the Lodges to be used for housing gardeners or other employees.

A club [which was] to include a library, common rooms, recreation rooms for men and women, billiard room, smoking room, dining room, kitchen and offices, lavatories for men and women, and quarters for a matron and caretaker ...

A hall to be placed close to 'Fox Oak'...to have seating accommodation for 500 persons and to include a stage and retiring rooms ...

A coal store, to be erected near the back entrance to the Park, so that coal for use in the Village could be purchased in bulk.

The Trustees had also confirmed their earlier decision to provide a church for the residents of the village, and Mr Walter Tapper was asked to submit sketch plans for '... a small Church to seat 300 ...'. When this became known there was a suggestion in the local press that the church should be built in conjunction with the development of St George's Hill, which had then just started, and this idea was in fact considered by the Trustees, but the Lord Bishop of London was strongly opposed to it, and it was quickly dropped. By March 1914, Mr Tapper had produced his plans for the church, and after some minor modifications these were approved, a limit of £5,000 being placed upon the cost of building it.

It is clear, from the outset, that the Trustees were determined to use the best materials that they could afford for the construction of the buildings in the village, and to make sure that all the work was carried out to a very high standard; a policy for which their successors have every reason to be grateful. Although they had been forced, on the grounds of cost, to accept some reductions in the quality of the materials to be used in the cottages, they were clearly determined to make no such compromise in respect of the church, as the following extracts from the specification drawn up for it illustrate:

Sand. The sand to be approved pit sand thoroughly washed and screened if necessary. It is to be clean sharp and silicious [sic] and entirely free from salt, clay, loam, dirt or organic matter of any description.

Cement. The cement to be Portland of best approved make and to answer the requirements of the British Standard Specification.

Concrete. The concrete in all cases to be mixed on a clean stone or wood floor and the water to be put on from a rose of a watering pot or hose. The whole mixture to be turned over twice before water is added and twice afterwards and to be laid at once and well beaten down and brought to a true level surface. The concrete to be laid continuously and no portion allowed to set before the rest is proceeded with. No traffic will be allowed over any portion of the concrete until thoroughly set. The trenches to be clear of water before the concrete is put in.

The timbers to be all from an approved port and best quality fir, or that known in the trade as 'Firsts'. No American, Swedish, or Scotch Fir will be allowed and no spruce.

The whole is to be cut die square of full specified dimensions and without waney [irregular] edges. Where necessary timbers are to be cut out of baulk.

All timber is to be free from sap, shakes, large, loose or dead knots and other defects, and is to be perfectly seasoned.

All work is to be properly framed together with all spikes, bolts, nails and other fixings, and to include for best workmanship and which if not actually specified is in any way implied.

The Oak to be of English growth, cut wainscot, felled at least 3 years, free from all defects, carefully selected for grain, seasoned properly and put together in

Joinery in most perfect manner, draw bored and pinned with Oak pins and where visible to be wrot [sic] free from stains and framed with Mason's joints.

The finished surface of the oak is to be thoroughly damped with a sponge and lime rubbed in about the consistency of cream, then brushed against the grain with a wire brush and afterwards well rubbed in with a hard bristle brush. Nothing but this treatment is required for finishing.

Another amenity which the Trustees decided should be provided was a recreation ground, and in early 1914 Messrs Carter & Co., seed merchants of Raynes Park, were engaged to prepare a report for them showing how the area allotted for this purpose could best be laid out '... for cricket, football and tennis grounds, and possibly a bowling green ...'. At the same time the Trustees went to the trouble to pass a formal resolution to the effect that Mr Bartlett, who was still acting as the Trustees' forestry adviser, should not be asked to advise on this project, which indicates that the earlier difference of opinion with him over his work on the Lime Avenue had not been entirely forgotten. Shortly afterwards, Messrs Carter & Co. produced their report, and were instructed to proceed as quickly as possible with the work they had recommended under the supervision of Mr Cave. It is notable that the Trust records covering this period make no mention whatever of who the Trustees intended should use this recreation ground, but the inclusion of a football pitch suggests that they did not have the villagers solely in mind!

When work on the clearings first began, the horses needed to help carry out the work were hired. By the end of 1913 this was costing at least 10s. (50p) a day, and Mr Cave suggested that it would be more economical to buy two horses than to continue hiring them. Sir Edward Ward, who was then permanent Under-Secretary of State for War, '... undertook to purchase a couple of good strong military casters not more than 7 or 8 years old which were too slow for military service at an estimated cost of £10 apiece'. This arrangement fell through, however, because the ex-military horses that were available proved to be unsuitable for the work. So, early in 1914, Mr Cave looked elsewhere and found some others which were suitable, although he had to pay £40 apiece for them. Two carts and a timber whim (winch), together with the necessary harness, were bought at the same time.

Having previously decided, at the time of the purchase of Fox Oak in May 1912, that they did not need a motor-car, the Trustees soon changed their minds when Mr Ingram told them how much was being spent on taxi fares to and from Walton-on-Thames railway station, not only for themselves, but for all the surveyors, consultants, assistants and others who needed to visit the estate on Trust business. Mr Ingram was accordingly told to purchase a second-hand car for the Trust in consultation with Mr Frank Whiteley, and to engage the services of a chauffeur. They first considered a six-cylinder Siddeley-Daisy limousine, but this was rejected because '... it was felt that a car of this size and character was not at the present stage really suitable for the requirements of The Trust and it was felt that the kind of car that was wanted was something in the way of a small car for entirely local use at Burhill'. Mr William Whiteley then '... mentioned a small second-hand Clement-Talbot car of which he knew as being for sale ...' and it was decided to leave all the arrangements for the purchase of a car to him and his brother in conjunction with Mr Ingram. They bought this car early in January 1913 for £75, and Mr Robert Coote was engaged as chauffeur at a wage of 23s. (£1.15) per week plus free lodging, which was provided for him in the stables at Fox Oak. He was also provided with a suit of livery. As the car had no lights, a pair of acetylene headlights were purchased and fitted (though apparently no rear lights) together with a set of tools, a dashboard mirror, and '... an iron box for storing petrol'.

This car did not turn out to be a good buy. In February permission had to be given for the purchase of two new tyres and inner tubes '... at a total cost not exceeding £17 ...' and then in July the back axle broke, costing £15 to repair. In November the speedometer broke and had to be completely replaced, as it was worn out. That cost £3 10s. (£3.50). Then a further £19 3s. (£19.15) had to be spent the following January to replace the other two tyres and tubes. Just over a month later Mr Ingram reported to the Trustees '... that the car shewed signs of decay ...' and asked for instructions. The Trustees had had enough, and told him to carry out any essential repairs preparatory to selling it whilst looking for a replacement.

The question had also arisen as to whether the car could be used by Mr Ingram and Mr Hennell (the Secretary and Assistant Secretary) for private purposes when it was not required for Trust business. When this was first put to The Trustees '... it was resolved to defer decision on this question and that pending decision the car should not be used otherwise than for official purposes but that the action of the Secretary in having previously given the Assistant Secretary permission to use the car for private purposes should be approved'. Later, the Trustees agreed to let Mr Ingram

13. The Trustees' horses.

14.   The car.

and Mr Hennell use the car for their private purposes '... when absolutely necessary ...', provided they kept a record of when they did so.

The acquisition of a motor-car soon revealed that the exit from Fox Oak Drive on to Seven Hills Road was dangerous, because it was concealed from the view of the drivers of cars coming from the direction of Cobham. The Trustees therefore proposed to erect a warning sign '... recommended by the AA ...' on the other side of the road at a cost of 27s. 6d. (£1.37) and, although the local council agreed to this, the owner of the property (including the verges) opposite Fox Oak, Mr Herbert Wood, objected. As a compromise, the sign was erected on the Trust's side of the road, with the addition of '... a hand pointing in the direction of the drive'.

During this period, the Trustees had their first dealings with the Charity Commissioners, to whom the Trust's annual accounts had to be submitted. Early in 1913 the Commissioners wrote to the Trustees asking for information as to what was being done, and Sir Arthur Boscawen, who had served as a Commissioner, was deputed to help the Secretary formulate a suitable reply. This consisted merely of a brief statement '... of what had been, was being and was proposed to be done together with a copy of the Block Plan ...'. Not surprisingly, this elicited a further enquiry from the Commissioners asking for more details, but the Trustees appear to have resented this and, in response to the second inquiry, 'Resolved that no further action should be taken beyond sending a formal acknowledgement'. When, in early 1914, the Commissioners wrote again suggesting that the Trustees '... should for their own protection [sic] submit [to them] the plans of the Cottages to be erected', they decided not to do so.

There were also during this period problems of a more mundane nature. Early in 1912 it was found that considerable damage was being done to the estate by deer, which were thought to have escaped from Ashley Park, and advice was sought as to the legal position if steps were taken to kill them. No further action appears to have been taken about deer at that time, although a little later that year Mr Ingram was told to take steps to keep the rabbits down, as they were proving to be a nuisance. Then on the night of Sunday, 22 February 1914, Fox Oak was broken into through one of the boardroom windows. When this was discovered, the police were called, but it was found that nothing of importance had been taken, and it was thought to be more likely the work of a passing tramp than of anyone employed on the estate.

An early decision by the Trustees was that a memorial to the founder should be erected at a central point in the village. In July 1912 they asked Mr Cave to approach Sir George Frampton RA '... with a view to obtaining terms for a Statue ...' and to report initially to Messrs William and Frank Whiteley for their approval. The Trustees' initial intention was clearly that this memorial should take the form of a statue of the founder, Mr William Whiteley, but Sir George Frampton had other ideas, and proposed that '... instead of a seated or standing figure [of Mr Whiteley] the base of the memorial should be surmounted by a symbolical figure and that a bust of the founder should be on the pedestal ...'. A little surprisingly, perhaps, this proposal met with the approval of the two sons, and was accordingly agreed to by the remainder of the Trustees.

In late October 1913 Mr Cave produced '... a sketch model [sic] of the Memorial prepared by Sir George Frampton consisting of a seated figure of Industry with a plaque on the front of the pedestal'. This was approved, subject to the inclusion of decoration on the reverse side of the pedestal '... in order to relieve the plainness of the effect presented by the back of the figure and the pedestal ...' and the sum of £4,000 was allocated for the work to be carried out. However, when the revised sketch model was produced a month later, the Trustees were still not satisfied, and asked for a full-sized template to be prepared to give them a better idea of what it would look like. When they saw this in position, they decided to broaden the pedestal, and to raise the whole memorial by building steps leading up to it around the base. It was also decided to incorporate a foundation stone in the base of the memorial, the stone to be hollow, and to contain '... a small plan of the Octagon to be prepared by the Consulting Architect and giving the names of the Architects ...'.

This foundation stone was laid by the Chairman of the Trustees at a simple ceremony held on Tuesday, 21 July 1914. The building of Whiteley Village had officially begun.

Chapter Four

BUILDING WHITELEY VILLAGE (1914-17)

At first, the building of the village proceeded rapidly, and by September 1914 the roads had all been mapped out, most of them had been roughly laid, the foundations of a good number of the blocks of cottages had been dug and walls were beginning to rise. In addition, the pond had been drained, and the foundations of the bridge which was to span it were being laid. Indeed, the building work was progressing at such a rate that Mr Cave, the consulting architect, felt it necessary to press the Trustees for a rapid decision about the plans for the electric mains and internal telephone systems so that the necessary wiring could be installed in the cottages before the builders plastered the walls.

On 4 August 1914, however, Great Britain declared war on Germany. The effect of this on the availability of labour and materials was quickly felt, and the very next month Henry Martin Ltd. approached Mr Cave suggesting the complete suspension of building works for the duration of the war or, failing that, a substantial increase to the agreed contract price in order to cover anticipated extra costs. The Trustees, for their part, were determined to keep the work going, and it is very much to their credit that they succeeded in doing so throughout the war, despite all the difficulties that arose. They therefore rejected out of hand the suggestion that the work should be suspended, agreed to consider proposals for justified price increases on their merits as they arose, and also agreed to extend the time limits allowed for the completion of the work where this could be shown to be justified.

Meanwhile, the initial adverse reaction to the outbreak of war having been overcome, work continued to proceed apace. In response to Cave's request, the electrical specifications of Mr Wilkinson, the consultant electrical engineer, were rapidly completed, and put out to tender. Six companies submitted tenders, as follows:

Rashleigh & Phipps	£3,997
Leo Sunderland & Co.	£3,300
Blackburn, Starling & Co. of Nottingham	£3,359
Pinching & Walton	£1,891
Edmundson's Electricity Corporation	£2,160
H. J. Cash & Co.	£2,047

Mr Wilkinson advised the Trustees to accept the tender from H. J. Cash & Co., but they went against his advice and awarded the contract to Pinching & Walton. Subsequently, they discovered that they had made a mistake, and asked for another £100. This was agreed to by the Trustees as it still left them with the lowest tender. However, by May 1915, as a result of the shortage of skilled labour and the rising cost of materials, they were forced to withdraw from their contract, which was then taken on by H. J. Cash & Co.

15.   The dry pond.

16.   Construction of the main sewer.

17-20. Building works, July 1914.

Building work continued throughout the remainder of 1914 and by the end of the year North Lodge, the bridge, and many of the cottages were beginning to take shape. Roofs were appearing on a number of cottages, and some more trees had been cleared, although it was felt by the Trustees that Mr Bartlett (the Forester) had once again been over-enthusiastic in clearing the woodland to the south of Fox Oak and had left the area somewhat bare. He was instructed to remedy this by replanting rhododendrons from elsewhere on the estate. By the end of the year, the Trustees had also approved the site for the village hall and for the church. Initially, it was proposed that this should be on the eastern side of North Avenue (where Whiteley House and the village hospital are today), but the Trustees considered that the other side of the road would be better. At this time, they also decided that North and South Avenues should be the only openings radiating from the monument in which roads should be laid, and that all the other openings should be grassed over. This undoubtedly gave the village a much more rural aspect than would otherwise have been the case.

By the end of the year, the Trustees had also approved the arrangements for the street lighting within the village, to consist partly of standard lamps and partly of lamps mounted on cottage walls by means of brackets. It was agreed that these should all be operated by one main switch. The water mains for the village had also necessitated a good deal of consideration, particularly to ensure that they would provide an adequate supply in case of fire, a matter on which expert advice was taken.

Early in January 1915 there was a severe gale which blew down or made dangerous many of the trees on the estate. Mr Bartlett was instructed to proceed with clearing the trees which had blown down and with felling and clearing those which were dangerous. He was also authorised to proceed with a plan he had put forward for the creation of an allotment patch, and for preparing the ground by bastard trenching it.

In March 1915, Henry Martin Ltd. submitted a report to the Trustees showing that, at the end of 1914, they had been between seven and eight weeks behind their contract schedule. It was agreed that this was fully justified. In May, however, they reported a further delay in fulfilling their contract due to a building strike in Northampton, where the firm was based. Nevertheless, work continued quite well throughout the year; by July West Lodge was completed ready for wiring, and by November a number of cottages had been fully completed, four of which had been furnished by Whiteley's (who else?) for the Trustees to inspect with a view to them deciding whether furnishings should be provided by the Trust or by the residents themselves. Discussion on this matter went on for several months. Finally, it was agreed to provide the cupboards and dressers which have remained an attractive feature of all the cottages up to the present day, together with curtain rods and curtains, a kitchen fender, and shelves and hooks in the scullery.

As work on the cottages progressed, discussion amongst the Trustees continued on a number of related topics. The question of coal storage was one of these. It had originally been intended to provide a one-hundredweight coal-bin in each cottage; then it was thought that it would be more economical to provide a larger bin of

21-26. Building works, December 1914.

three-to four-hundredweight capacity so as to reduce the number of coal deliveries required. The difficulty with this plan was that there simply was not enough room inside the cottages for such a large bin. It was accordingly decided to provide creosoted wooden bins of just over four-hundredweight capacity outside the back doors of cottages, or, for first-floor cottages, on the landings outside the front door 'where space allowed'. It was also decided to build a substantial coal store near the back entrance in Chestnut Avenue.

Another topic on which discussion continued was that of the proper provision for nurses' cottages within the sections, this being a matter on which the Trustees had previously changed their minds on a number of occasions. In March, as a result of inspecting the site, they decided not only to dispense with the proposed 'isolation cottage' but to dispense with the proposed nurses' cottages in North Avenue and South Avenue. Later that year, Sir Aston Webb, drawing on his experience as chairman of the 'Homes for the Aged Poor' in London, advised against this reduction, and the Trustees, acting on his advice, changed their minds yet again, and decided to retain the principle of providing accommodation for nurses in each section so that each section would have a nurse on duty.

During 1915 progress was also made with the hall, the church, and the central monument. The contract for the construction of the hall, which had been designed by Sir Aston Webb, was placed with Henry Martin at a cost of £5,564, plus an additional £250 for the construction of a retaining wall to support the carriage drives leading up to it. To these sums had to be added another £232 for the clock, which was built by Gillett & Johnston of Croydon. The specification for this was that it should have four faces, and should strike the hours and quarters. Henry Martin Ltd. were also awarded the contract for building the church at a total cost of £9,241 3s. and work began. A clay model of the central monument had been completed in March by Sir George Frampton and approved by the Trustees. In June, however, it was discovered that the word 'MUNIFICENT' on the stone plinth for the monument had been misspelled, the 'F' having been carved as an 'E'. This was corrected by having the base of the 'E' filled in. The permanence of this method of repair was questioned, but nothing further was done. At the time of writing, the mistake is just becoming visible again. By October, the memorial figure had been completed. The contractors were anxious to have it removed, because they needed the space for munitions work, and so the Trustees decided to have it '... set up on the pedestal and boarded up and otherwise adequately protected until the time came for the opening ceremony'.

In June the Trustees were told that the gates were almost complete, despite the war effort. On the other hand, they were also told that the contract for the laying of the main electric mains had been delayed by about five to six weeks because of shortage of materials due to the war, and Cash & Co. (who had by then taken over the internal electrical wiring contract from Pinching & Walton) were asking for their contract to be revised to cover increased costs resulting from the war. It would seem that in 1915 the effect of the war on the supply of materials was beginning to be felt, but was not yet really serious. The negotiations with the water company were also brought to a satisfactory conclusion, it being agreed that:

27. Building the village hall.

28. The foundations for St Mark's.

... the Company should supply the whole of the water required by the Trustees by meter and covenant to supply it so long as required at 9d. per 1,000 gallons throughout, the Trustees having the right to terminate the arrangement at any time by giving 6 months notice so that if the Trustees were dissatisfied at any time or decided to take some other supply they were free to do so.

On the estate, the sports field continued to be a problem. Carters Ltd. were still trying to rid it of weeds and agreed to bear half the cost of this, employing six women for eight weeks to tackle the task. As regards the lake, although the Trustees had originally planned to expand and deepen it, the cost of doing so proved to be much higher than expected. They accordingly decided to do no more than make it watertight and tidy it up; this alone cost £776 10s. 0d.

As 1915 drew to a close, the effects of the war began to be more seriously felt. Lord Derby's appeal of 4 December calling on every available man to express his willingness to serve his country, whether or not his employer thought his services indispensable, set the tone. Mr Hennell, the Assistant Secretary, told the Trustees he felt obliged to respond. They accepted this, but told him that they intended to appeal when his unit was called up.

In March 1916 Mr Hennell was called up, together with several other Trust employees. If any appeal was made to retain Mr Hennell's services, it was obviously not allowed, as the Trustees had to arrange for Mr Lawson, the secretary of Burhill Golf Club, to take over as Assistant Secretary, and to make various other staff changes to fill the posts which had been vacated. In January 1916 the contract of Mr Cave, who had been ill the previous year, expired and was not renewed.

Then, in April, the Ministry of Munitions wrote to the Secretary querying the necessity of the work being done and the labour being employed. A satisfactory reply was obviously given, as at that time the Ministry lodged no objection to the work continuing. However, they raised the matter again later in the year, making it clear that a licence would be needed for any further construction. The Trustees nevertheless decided to continue with the work in hand, although they realised that a licence might not be granted and could result in serious consequences for them. In October, the Ministry raised the question again, and Sir Edward Coates, Sir Walpole Greenwell, Arthur Ingram, the Secretary, and Sir Aston Webb attended a meeting with a Mr Johnston, the Secretary to the Ministry of Munitions, at which they explained the importance of continuing the building work. Mr Johnston asked to be allowed to see for himself what was being done, and did so in December. As a result of this visit the necessary licence was granted early the following year.

Throughout 1916 building work progressed steadily. Indeed, by February it was decided that as work was already so far advanced in section F that efforts should be concentrated on that section in order to get it completed and actually in use within the next few months.

A major problem that was encountered over the winter of 1915/16 was that of drainage and of making sure that the foundations of cottages were not flooded. A variety of remedial works were put in hand, some at considerable extra expense. As a result of the need to carry out these remedial works, it was decided in April that instead of the F section cottages opening first, Sir Aston Webb's cottages in E Section should be the first to open as these were free from damp. It was estimated that they would be ready by the end of July. It is worth noting that, at that stage in the development of the village, the eight sections then under construction were already being called by the letters A to H, as they are to this day. In July 1915 a proposal had been made to name the Sections, but nothing came of it. It was Mr Ingram who proposed in a letter to Mr Gillett (a Trustee) dated 9 February 1915, that the village should be called 'Whiteley Village' and that was the name by which it became known, although no firm decision was made at that time.

By May 1916 the contractors, Faulkeners, reported that they had completed the gas mains, and that the gas company had officially approved their work. The gas company, however, had proved unwilling to rent meters to the Trust, and the Trustees decided that the Trust should buy and install its own meters. Everything concerned with the distribution of gas within the village therefore became the responsibility of the Trust.

In June 1916 a strange letter was received from a Sapper Alliborne, who was stationed in Llandudno, alleging that 'certain charges were being wrongly made in the accounts sent in by the builders'. The Trustees decided to ask Lt Philip Webb, RE, who was also stationed at Llandudno at that time and who was the son and partner of Sir Aston Webb, to interview Sapper Alliborne about his allegations. The minutes of a meeting of the Finance Committee held about a month later on 26 July record that, as a result of a letter from Sir Aston Webb (presumably containing news of the interview between his son and Sapper Alliborne), the Secretary had had an interview with Mr Smith of Henry Martin Ltd., the result of which was that no further action would be taken but that '... the matter would be kept in mind'. Nothing further was heard from Sapper Alliborne, and Lt Webb was unfortunately killed in France three months later. The matter was not referred to again.

The estimated completion date of the end of July 1916 for the first batch of cottages proved over-optimistic, and had to be postponed until '... after the winter'. Even this was to prove over-optimistic. By February 1917 the position was as follows:

Sir Aston Webb's and Mr Atkinson's cottages in F section were all but ready.

Sir Aston Webb's and Mr McCartney's cottages in E section would, it was thought, be ready in about six weeks' time.

Mr McCartney's and Sir Ernest George's Cottages in D section were estimated to need another 10 weeks.

The drainage works needed in Chestnut Avenue would, it was estimated, take some considerable time yet, and the approach road (the back entrance) past the coal bunkers and to the shop, at least another six months.

The Trustees now hoped that they would be able to open the first three blocks of cottages by 1 June 1917 at the latest, but these estimates were based on the assumption that there would be no further deterioration in the labour or supply situations. However, in March of that year the Defence of the Realm (National Service Order) was promulgated, restricting the employment of men aged between 18 and 61. Although the Trustees wrote to the Director General of National Service requesting a ruling as to whether or not the Trust came under the terms of this Order '... or was to be regarded as a work of National importance, especially in view of the Licence granted to the Trustees to proceed with the development given by the Ministry of Munitions ...', there is nothing to show that the Trust was accorded any measure of exemption from the Order. In any event, the Trustees decided to proceed as quickly as they could with the opening of as many blocks of cottages as possible, and to recruit: a matron and two nurses, the choice of a medical adviser being deferred; an engineer foreman, who would also look after the Trust's vehicles; two handymen, to deal with the coal supply; and a chaplain.

In addition, it was decided that, as a preliminary, an advertisement should be drawn up and a copy sent to all those who had applied for the benefits of the charity before sending a more formal notice and application form to those who replied to the advertisement. As a result of this, in June 1917 the secretary sent out 376 application forms, of which 132 were not returned. Of those which were returned:

78 initially seemed suitable (including 30 OAPs).

44 others (probably suitable) were dependent on the old age pension.

29 were 'doubtful'.

65 said they did not wish to apply.

23 wanted their applications deferred.

Two were reported, by those replying on their behalf, as having died.

Three were ineligible, due to having excess income.

For those applicants wishing to come and see the village, the Trustees decided that the Trust should pay their third-class return rail fare, but not the cost of conveyance to and from Walton station.

Advertisements for the post of 'Lady Superintendent' (which title had been agreed upon instead of 'Matron') were placed in *The Times*, the *Morning Post*, the *Daily Telegraph*, *The Lancet* and the *British Medical Journal* at a salary of £150 a year. Five hundred and fifty applications were received, from which 12 had been short-listed. These were considered on 27 July 1917 by a committee consisting of Sir Walpole Greenwell and Sir Edward Coates, which recommended that a Miss Gabbett be appointed.

Miss Gabbett attended a full meeting of the Trustees on 26 September, at which her appointment was confirmed, it being finally decided to call her the 'Lady Warden'. At that meeting it was also decided:

That she should temporarily reside in Fox Oak.

That one of the cottages should be provided for her use as a temporary office and dispensary.

That she should engage a cook and a housemaid as her servants at an average wage not exceeding £25 per annum each, these wages to be paid by the Trust.

To appoint, on the recommendation of Miss Gabbett, Miss Furley of 'Grata Quies' military hospital, a qualified nurse, to act as the Lady Warden's assistant at a salary of £100 per annum plus fuel and light, and free accommodation in a cottage.

To engage, also on Miss Gabbett's recommendation, Mrs Reynolds, a nurse, to act as a general help, at a salary of £1 per week plus similar allowances, with accommodation in a cottage.

By early October 1917, the stage had at last been reached when things were ready for the first villagers to take up residence in the village. The first actually to do so was Miss Eliza Palmer, a retired nurse, who moved into 96 Octagon Road (F10) on Wednesday, 10 October 1917. Although many of the facilities were either rudimentary or lacking altogether, and there was still a great deal to be done, the life of Whiteley Village as a community had begun.

Chapter Five

LIFE IN THE VILLAGE IN THE EARLY YEARS (1917-21)

Two other villagers also moved into their new cottages on 10 October 1917, Mrs Sarah Allen to E2 and Mrs Mary Murphy to E25; Miss Palmer's claim to be the first of these three being based upon a note in her record which reads 'Gave her a Bible as a memento of being the first to enter'. By the end of the month, another 25 new villagers had joined them, as follows:

11 October: Mrs Dench to E18
13 October: Mrs Cook to E24
16 October: Mr Scholey (the first man) to E17
                 Mr and Mrs Dudley (the first married couple) to E21
17 October: Miss Margaret Plaice and Miss Bessie Plaice, who were sisters, to F11
                 Miss Climpson to F6
                 Miss Ogier to E16
18 October: Miss Tribe to E26
                 Miss Ratcliff to E23
20 October: Mrs Bone to E20
22 October: Mrs Mee to E3
24 October: Mr and Mrs Shaw to E22
26 October: Mrs Bills to E28
                 Miss Langley to E27
27 October: Miss Furrell to E19
                 Mr and Mrs Pittman to E15
                 Mr Spurll to F1
31 October: Miss Calf to F17
                 Mrs Chapple to F2
                 Miss Furrell (whose sister had moved into E19 on 27th) to F4
                 Mrs Mayo to E29

The arrival of new villagers continued slowly. By the end of the year there were still only 42 in residence and, although from May 1918 onwards the cottages in C and D sections progressively became ready for occupation, by the end of that year there were still only 94 villagers, 96 having been admitted and two having died.

Throughout this period it was Miss Gabbett, the newly-appointed Lady Warden, who ran the village, and she was undoubtedly faced with many problems. In the first place, the village was still really little more than a building site, with a great deal of construction work still going on. The grounds had not yet been laid out, and amenities were few.

In November 1917, as a result of a proposal by Miss Gabbett, a communal kitchen was established for the benefit of villagers and female members of staff. This was intended as a temporary war-time measure to help overcome the shortages of some types of food which were beginning to be felt, and to help ease the burden for those concerned by the effect of rising prices. The plan was that the kitchen should pay for itself, and a cook, Bridget Nolan, was appointed at a salary of 15s. (75p) per week. The kitchen was located in the present stores building.

In early 1917 a small village shop was established in the hall, and in late 1917 this was moved to its present site. At first this was run almost as a branch of Whiteley's in Bayswater; they supplied all the provisions (to be sold at their London prices!) as well as supplying the staff to run it, except for the storekeeper who was a member of the Trust staff. Later, in mid-1918, the running of the village stores was taken over by the Trust and Mr and Mrs Baker were appointed to be responsible for running both the stores and the communal kitchen, which had by then become a sort of canteen.

To help her in running the village, Miss Gabbett had a staff consisting of nurses, painters, plumbers, labourers, storekeepers, clerks, a chauffeur, cooks, maids and ex-Sergeant Luby, who acted as night-watchman. The services of a chaplain, church organist, doctor and dentist were also available. In addition she had Mr Comport, who, having acted as clerk of works in the early stages of the construction of the village, was appointed the first works manager. Mr Thomas Edwards was the head

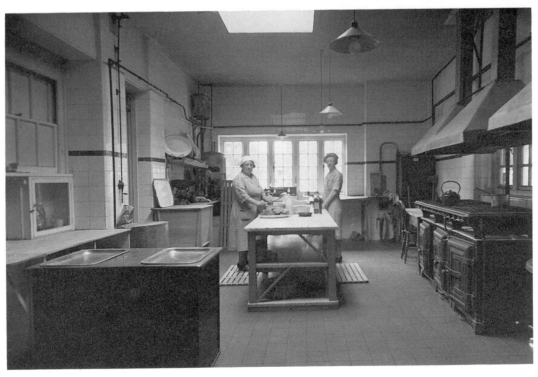

29.　The communal kitchen.

30. Mr H. E. Cook, the first warden.

gardener and a little later, on 30 June 1920, at the age of 61, he and Miss Ella Mary Jones became the first couple to be married in St Mark's church, after which she took up residence with him in West Lodge. At that time most of the Trust staff were living in the village, and Fox Oak was used as the administrative centre for the village as well as a home for Mr H. E. Cooke, who was appointed as the first 'Agent and General Manager' to the Trustees in March 1919, and took over from Miss Gabbett the overall responsibility for running the village and the estate. Unfortunately, later that year Miss Gabbett was forced to retire due to ill-health and Mrs Chapman, who had for some months been helping her, was appointed as Lady Warden, a post she held until 1937. Mr Cooke was the first of only three 'Wardens' (as they became known) appointed by the Trustees during the 67-year period covered by this book; a list of them is given in Appendix L.

After the end of the war in 1919, the village began to expand rapidly, and by 1 March 1920 there were 224 villagers and 35 members of staff. From early in 1919 the nurses' cottage in section A (10 Octagon Road) was used as a guest house for visitors and 'run on boarding house lines' [sic]. At about the same time, the nurses' cottage in section C (44 Octagon Road) was equipped as a temporary hospital while plans were drawn up to build a permanent hospital for the village. Mrs Chapman lived in the nurses' cottage in section F (67 and 67a Circle Road) while the nurses' cottage in Section B (17 Circle Road) was used as the chaplaincy.

St Mark's church was dedicated on St Mark's Day, 25 April 1918, at a service conducted by the Lord Bishop of Winchester, assisted by the Chairman of the Trustees, the Bishop of London, and the Revd E. Pelloe, vicar of St Peter's Hersham, who was then acting as village chaplain. The sermon was preached by one of the Trustees, the Bishop of Stepney. After the service, the small side-chapel was also dedicated. This was later used as a mortuary, but is now the village Roman Catholic chapel of the Most Holy Family. A list of the chaplains of St Mark's church is given at Appendix M.

31. St Mark's church.

The organist was Miss Green of Hersham; she had been engaged by the Trust with the additional responsibility of training the choir, which in part consisted of girls from Hersham. Services for Nonconformist villagers were at first held in the village hall, but during 1919 permission was given for them to hold their services in St Mark's on Sunday and Wednesday afternoons. This was probably the first example of the spirit of ecumenicism at work in the village. The Trustees, however, had recognised the need for a separate church to be provided for Nonconformist worship, but had decided not to build one until the war was over. At that time, the number of Roman Catholics living in the village was insufficient to justify any special provision for them, so arrangements were made to take them to and from the Roman Catholic church in Weybridge on Sundays and other holy days.

The social life of the village centred around the village hall. A village club was formed in 1918, and began to hold meetings there. At first, this was exclusively a men's club, but as the number of lady villagers already heavily outweighed the number of gentleman villagers (as it still does) the rules were quite quickly amended to include the ladies. Facilities for showing films were provided in the hall early in 1920, and a weekly show consisting of a news reel, feature and a comedy was screened. These were, of course, all silent films. Village bowls and cricket clubs were established in early 1921, and visiting teams made use of the recreation ground from late 1920 onwards.

The first edition of the village magazine was published in April 1919. This was a quarterly issue until 1921, when the Trustees decided to base the magazine on a widely-known monthly publication of the time called *The Dawn of Day* (which later

32.   The interior of St Mark's church.

became *The New Day*) published by the SPCK. The first edition of this new village magazine was published in May 1921, and consisted of *The Dawn of Day* enclosed within a locally produced cover headed 'Whiteley Village Magazine' which contained village notices and articles. The price was 2d. This format continued for many years. In September 1940, the name of the insert changed to *Church and Home* (which was subtitled 'Incorporating 'The New Day'') and this was used until January 1952 when a new insert entitled *Home Words* began to be used. The use of *Home Words* continued (although some monthly inserts seem to have been omitted) until the end of 1963. From January 1964 onwards, however, the village magazine has been entirely 'home produced' and provides a very valuable means of communication with the villagers and members of staff about all the things going on in the village.

By the end of 1918 almost all the building work that had been put in hand, including all the cottages, had been finished, but nothing new had been started since 1917, probably because of continuing shortages of labour and materials and the necessity of obtaining a specific licence from the Ministry of Munitions before beginning any new building work. It may also have seemed prudent at that time to let the village become established as a community and to allow a pattern of life to develop before deciding what further buildings were really needed. It was therefore not until 1919 that the Trustees began to discuss the need for any additional buildings. At a meeting held at Fox Oak on Saturday, 10 May that year, the Trustees decided to proceed with the building of:

A club house, to be situated next to the hall

An administrative block, to include both a rest home and a hospital opposite St Mark's church

33. Inside the village hall.

Three pairs of staff houses along Chestnut Avenue

Another pair of staff houses next to the hall (on the opposite side to the club)

Houses for the chaplain and Lady Warden next to St Mark's church

Later these plans were revised and, instead of building a pair of staff cottages next to the hall, the house for the Lady Warden was built there and only the house for the chaplain was built next to St Mark's. Henry Martin Ltd. were again awarded the contracts for this work in the sums of £18,830 for the rest home and hospital building and £5,533 for the club house. Then, in March 1920, the Trustees decided to avail themselves of the government grants that had become available, ranging from £130 to £160 (later increased to £250) per house, under the Housing (Additional Powers) Act of 1919 and to build three pairs of staff houses on the Nursery Fields site, now known as Combe Lane.

These new buildings had been begun by the end of 1919, but in May 1920 work had to be suspended for almost two months because of industrial action. By then the dispute had been brewing since March when the trade unions concerned claimed that London rates of pay should be paid with effect from 1 May to all those working on the new buildings in accordance with an agreement entered into between them and the employers. Henry Martin Ltd. made it clear that they were willing to pay the new rates, but would regard the additional cost as an 'authorised increase' which, within the terms of their current contracts, would have added about £5,000 to the cost of the work then in hand, and between 10 and 15 per cent to the cost of any future building work. The Trustees were understandably reluctant to agree to this. According to the definition of London District, specified in Clause II of the Working Rules between Masters and Men, Whiteley Village was 1½ miles outside the District. This fact was confirmed by the Chief Conciliation Officer, and the Trustees accordingly refused to pay the London rates with the result that on 24 May all building work stopped when the men went on strike in response to a call from their union. The strike lasted eight weeks, and work was not resumed until 19 July, as a result of a final ruling from the South Eastern Conciliation Board to the effect that Whiteley Village '... being within the Walton-on-Thames Urban District ... London Rates and Conditions apply to all work' – a ruling which the Trustees felt reluctantly obliged to accept.

In the summer of 1919 the Trustees turned their attention to the landscaping of the area surrounding the cottages, and Mr Inigo Triggs, a well-known landscape gardener, was engaged to plan and supervise the work. As a start, the roads and walks around the village were given names, '... the principle being that the main roads at right angles to the Monument be called Avenues ... and that the transverse ways bisecting these quadrants be called Walks'. All four of the walks were turfed and this turfing was continued into the areas between the walks and the monument within Circle Road. The remaining unturfed areas within the circle were edged with heather, and existing trees and shrubs were left in place. The entire length of the avenues were lined with trees, which continued in front of the cottages, with Scotch pines being used along the North and South Avenues and lime trees along East and West Avenues. The areas within the Sections of cottages were each laid out to a different design. In some cases existing trees and shrubs were left in place, while in others, allotments, fruit trees, lavender borders and thuja hedges were planted. A bowling green was laid down in F section, and there were also plans for an ornamental pond to be incorporated into one of the layouts. This idea was abandoned, however, and it is clear that not all Inigo Triggs' plans were actually carried out.

By early 1919 a definite pattern of village life had been established, as is shown by the following notices governing activities within the village which were sanctioned by the Trustees at a meeting held on 14 January of that year:

Church	St Mark's church Services at 8 a.m., 11 a.m. and 6.30 p.m. on Sundays. Free church services in the hall at 3.30 on Sunday and Wednesday afternoons.
Library	Lending library in the hall open on Saturday and Wednesday afternoons, 2.30-5 p.m.
Sewing party	Sewing party in the hall for mending for soldiers every Friday afternoon at 3 p.m.

Communal kitchen	Open daily (Sundays excepted)Dinners to be fetched in the following order: C section – 11.45 a.m.; E section – 12.05 p.m.; D section – 11.55 a.m.; F section – 12.15 p.m.
Market stores	Rationed articles supplied on Tuesdays in the following order: E & F Sections from 10 a.m.-12.30 p.m.; C & D sections from 2 p.m.-4 p.m.
Laundry	Soiled linen to be taken to Mrs Speller (Nurse Speller), section E8 on Tuesdays at 11 a.m.
Milk	The milkman arrives daily in the village at 10.30 a.m. and rings a bell as he comes to each section.
Baker	The baker calls at the market stores on Monday, Wednesday and Saturday, 11 a.m.-12 noon.

34.   The village bus (with Mr Coote at the wheel).

35.   Shopping at the village stores.

Village cart

The village cart leaves the monument at 9 a.m. on
Mondays for Walton station, returning at 4.30 p.m.
(By special request, if there be a party of four, the cart
will leave the monument at 7 a.m. in time to catch the
cheap 9d. return train to London at 7.45 p.m.) The
village cart leaves the monument for Walton village as
follows: Tuesday, 2 p.m. – for villagers in C section;
Wednesday, 9 p.m. – for villagers in D section; Thursday,
2 p.m. – for villagers in E section; Friday, 2 p.m. – for
villagers in F section. Tickets are necessary for any of
these journeys (price 2d.).

Lighting order   All lights to be out at 10 p.m. and are not to be lit until 6.30 a.m.

The village cart referred to in the notices was replaced in June of 1919 by a 12-seater 'La Buine' omnibus. By 1921 the village population had grown so much (and journeys to Walton had proved so popular) that the Trustees replaced the 'La Buine' with a 30-seater 'Lacre' omnibus.

Life in the village during this period is well described in a series of four articles entitled 'As it was in the Beginning' which were anonymously published in the village magazine early in 1949. These are reproduced in full at Appendix N.

By early 1921, the cottages were almost all occupied, and the new buildings were all but complete. Much of the work of laying-out the grounds had also been completed, yet there had still been no formal opening. As early as mid-1920 the Bishop of London had made enquiries about the possibility of the village being opened by a member of the royal family, and had been told that, although this would be unlikely, a royal visit might well be possible. Nothing more was heard until early in May 1921, when a letter was received from the Palace announcing that King George V and Queen Mary proposed to pay a visit to the village on Saturday, 28 May next! An emergency meeting of the Trustees was called at once. With less than four weeks' notice the Trustees had a multitude of arrangements to make. A programme for the visit had to be arranged and agreed, which included an itinerary. A special plan of the village was drawn up, and Whiteley's (who else?) were hired to cater for the royal party, the Trustees and their guests, as well as for the villagers and members of staff. Extra labourers were hired to make sure that everything was ship-shape, and local organisations contacted to help with lining the route. It must have been an extremely busy time for all concerned. All too soon, no doubt, the great day dawned. The story of the events of that day is best told in the words of the official report of the visit in the Trust records.

Chapter Six

A ROYAL VISIT

OFFICIAL REPORT OF THE ROYAL VISIT TO WHITELEY VILLAGE MADE BY THEIR MAJESTIES KING GEORGE V AND QUEEN MARY ON SATURDAY, 28th MAY 1921

Their Majesties reached the North Entrance by car at about 3.30 p.m. – having stopped en route at Thames Ditton to inspect a statue of the late King Edward.

In attendance on Their Majesties were Capt the Hon Alexander Hardinge MC, Equerry, and the Countess Fortescue, Lady-in-Waiting.

Awaiting their arrival at the Entrance were stationed the Lord Bishop of London, Chairman of the Trustees; Col the Hon Arthur Brodrick, Chairman of the Executive Committee; and Messrs William and Frank Ernest Whiteley, Trustees and sons of the Founder of the Trust; also Mr Herbert E. Cooke, the Agent and General Manager; and Capt Sant, Chief Constable of Surrey in charge of the Police arrangements.

The Bishop of London presented Messrs William and Frank Whiteley, Col Brodrick, Mr Cooke, and Capt Sant.

Miss Nora Whiteley, granddaughter of the Founder of the Trust was then presented, and Her Majesty was graciously pleased to accept from her a bouquet tendered on behalf of the Trust.

Mr Cooke received the Royal Command to take a seat by the side of the Chauffeur of the Royal car so that he might reply to Their Majesties' inquiries on the tour, which then took place with Messrs William and Frank Whiteley preceeding in their car, as pilot car, and the Bishop of London and Col Brodrick following the Royal car in the Bishop's car.

The procession went at a slow pace round the Octagon by the Eastern side, and then up the main road to and round the Monument. Their Majesties alighted to inspect it. Stationed there was Sir George Frampton RA, the Sculptor, with whom Their Majesties conversed.

Awaiting Their Majesties at the church, which was the next point to be visited, were The Bishop of London and Col Brodrick, who had left the procession at the end of the tour round the Octagon, and the following whom the Bishop of London presented in the following order: The Rt Hon Sir Arthur Griffith Boscawen, PC, MP, (Minister of Agriculture); Sir Edward Coates Bart MP and Mr William Edward Gillett – Trustees – also the Revd G E Pouncey, the Church of England (resident) Chaplain; Mr Walter Tapper, the Architect of the Church; and Mr Arthur D. Ingram, the Secretary to the Trust.

Within the church were the Organist and Girl Choir, the latter in their robes. The National Anthem was sung by the Choir, and thereafter Their Majesties were conducted round the building by the Bishop of London and the Chaplain, and called on Mr Tapper for information on points of Architectural detail.

36. The Bishop of London introducing Mr William Whiteley to Their Majesties at the north entrance.

After leaving the Church Their Majesties were graciously pleased to plant each a Swiss Pine on either side of the entrance to the Church yard from the North Avenue. Mr Inigo Triggs, Landscape Architect, who superintended the arrangements was presented. On duty were Mr Edwards, the Head Gardener and Mr J. Hickman, Foreman Gardener.

Their Majesties then crossed the road to the Homes of Rest in process of completion by the builders. Awaiting them there were the following who were presented by the Bishop of London:- Sir Bernard Greenwell Bart – Trustee – Sir Aston Webb

37. The Weybridge and Cobham Girl Guides saluting. The leading car is that of Mr William Whiteley piloting the royal car.

PRA, Consulting Architect, Sir John Oakley, Consulting Surveyor; and Mr Maurice Webb; also Mr Frank Comport (Works Manager) Clerk of Works.

Thence Their Majesties proceeded by car to the Hospital. Awaiting them there were the following who were presented:- The Bishop of Stepney – Trustee – Mrs Chapman, the Lady Warden, and Dr Sparks, the Medical Officer. On duty in the Hospital were:- Sister Shelton and Sister Greene, also Nurse Baker and Miss Virgo (cook).

A tour was made of the Wards, and Their Majesties shook hands and conversed with all patients who were well enough. While at the Hospital Their Majesties asked the Bishop of London whether there were children resident in the Village, and learning that the Lady Warden had a little son sent for Master Jack Chapman, who had the honour of being presented.

After leaving the Hospital the Royal Car proceeded to the Stores, Kitchen and Post Office block. By inadvertance the Bishop's car took the wrong direction and Col Brodrick, alighting, proceeded on foot and received Their Majesties on arrival. The following, who had been awaiting there, were presented to Their Majesties by the Bishop of London within the building:- The Rt Hon Herbert Pike Pease MP (Assistant Postmaster General) and Miss Dorothy Egerton – Trustees – also Mr Frank Atkinson, the designer of the lay-out of the Octagon. Mr Walter Cave, the Architect of the building was also presented. On duty at the Stores and Post Office were Mr & Mrs Mundy, and Mrs Theobald (Assistant) and at the Kitchen Sister Bowden, Nurse

38.   The Bishop of London introducing Trustees to His Majesty outside St Mark's. Left to right: Revd G. E. Pouncey (chaplain); Sir Arthur Griffith Boscawen; Sir Edward Coates, Bt, MP; Mr Gillett; His Majesty; the Bishop of London; Mr Frank Whiteley.

39.   Leaving St Mark's.

40. Procession from the church headed by Captain Sant (Chief Constable of Surrey).

Speller, Miss Bridget Nolan (Cook), and Miss Edith Caswell (Kitchen Maid). Their Majesties graciously accepted picture postcards of the Village.

Their Majesties and the party then proceeded on foot under the guidance of the Agent & General Manager and Lady Warden to inspect the Cottages of the following villagers:- Mr (formerly Assistant Supt of School Attendance Offices under the LCC) & Mrs Moon, 4 West Avenue; Mr Arthur Thomas Kennison, 11 West Avenue, pensioner of the Surrey Constabulary; and Miss Eliza Palmer, 96 Octagon Road, the first villager admitted. Their Majesties then proceeded on foot to the Hall, where were awaiting them the following, who were presented by the Lord Bishop of London:- The Rev W Thomas, non-Conformist Minister; the Rev Father Henly, Roman Catholic Priest; and Mr H D Wilkinson, Consulting Engineer. They called for and conversed with Mr Daniel Scholey, Crimean Veteran and Greenwich Pensioner who was a Villager.

Miss Bishop, a Villager, had entertained the company pending Their Majesties' arrival with a selection on the piano.

Thereafter Mr William Whiteley presented his co-directors Mr John Lawrie, the Managing Director and Mr J L Bushnell, Mr F G Dann and Col Sir Courtauld Thomson, who was also a Trustee; and at His Majesty's request Mr Lawrie presented

41.   The King planting a tree near the church. Mr Edwards, head gardener, is holding the tree in position.

25 representatives of the staff of the firm whose average length of service exceeded 40 years.

The Village Choral Society, composed entirely of Villagers, and accompanied on the piano by Miss May, a Villager, rendered the glee 'May Day' – by Muller – and the National Anthem. His Majesty was pleased to remark to the Lady Warden that he considered the performance wonderful.

Their Majesties then proceeded on foot to the Club House. A gilded key was presented to His Majesty on behalf of the Trust by Mr Frank Comport (Works Manager) who had been Clerk of Works of all buildings from the inception of development, and His Majesty formally opened the building for use for the first time.

Within tea had been prepared for Their Majesties; and, in another part of the building for the Trustees' guests. Their Majesties partook. The following persons received the Royal Command:- Mr William and Mr Frank Whiteley, the Bishop of London and Col Brodrick, and Capt Sant. The party was arranged at three tables – His Majesty with Mr Frank Whiteley and the Bishop at one; Her Majesty with Mr William Whiteley and Col Brodrick at the second; and Capt Sant joined Capt Hardinge and the Countess Fortescue at the third.

On leaving the Club House His Majesty observed Sir David Wilson KCMG (one of the Trustees' guests) ex-governor of Honduras, who as acting Governor of Trinidad had entertained His Majesty when, as Prince of Wales, he had visited the Island, and Their Majesties conversed with him.

Their Majesties then entered their car to depart, having expressed themselves to the Chairman of the Trustees as extremely pleased with all they had seen at the Village.

The Depot Band of the Queen's Royal Regiment (West Surrey) which had been stationed on The Green throughout the visit, played the National Anthem.

The Royal car was piloted to the West Entrance by Messrs William and Frank Whiteley in their car.

The time of departure was about 5.15 p.m.

The Trustees' guests and the Press (269) partook of tea at the Club House, and Villagers and Staff and others (598) in the Hall. Tea for Chauffeurs (50) was provided at the Minor Buildings.

In addition to the Surrey Constabulary who were on duty on the line of route and elsewhere, there were in attendance throughout members of the Staff of the Trust and Messrs Martin's foreman (builders) acting as Stewards: and the Weybridge Girl Guides and Walton-on-Thames Boy Scouts lined the route and positioned at various points during the visit.

Chapter Seven

THE VILLAGE IN THE '20s AND '30s (1922-38)

The village was now officially open, and, although they undoubtedly intended to expand it over the next few years, the Trustees decided that this was an appropriate juncture at which to prepare a memorandum recording what they called 'The Foundation of the Scheme of the Trust'. The Trust records state that:

> The Object of this Memorandum is in the lifetime of some of the original Trustees to place on record for the benefit of future Trustees and others interested the considerations and circumstances which influenced the Trustees in Founding the Scheme as developed up to the time the village was opened and other points of interest.

This memorandum was published in November 1922 and is reproduced in full in Appendix O.

As the club house, rest home and new staff houses described in chapter five were gradually completed, the Trustees again began to consider not only what additional buildings were required for the proper running of the village, but also the possibility of increasing the size of the village by building more cottages for villagers. By 1922, however, the Trust's capital had been substantially depleted by the costs already incurred in the purchase of the site and the building and equipping of the village up to that time. During that period a series of 'development statements' had been regularly produced for the Trustees showing the costs incurred so far, and the last of these, dated 24 June 1922, is reproduced in full in Appendix P. From the statement it will be seen that the following expenditure had been incurred up to that date:

Cost of site plus Fox Oak	£47,900 8s. 0d.
All other building and development costs	£415,329 6s. 9d.
Total	£463,229 14s. 9d.

The Trustees, therefore, had only just over half the original bequest left at that juncture. To understand the financial position in which they found themselves, it needs to be borne in mind that the running of the village as it already stood was undoubtedly their first priority, and that the cost of this had to be met wholly from the income derived from the investment of the remaining capital, because not only did the villagers of that time pay neither rent nor any other charge for their cottages, they also received a free allowance of coal and had their gas and electricity paid for

42. An aerial view of the village in 1922.

by the Trust. In addition, many villagers were in receipt of a cash allowance from the Trust to ensure that they were receiving the minimum levels of income set by the Trustees of 12s. 6d. (62½p) a week for single persons and 10s. (50p) a week each for married couples. Any further substantial reduction of the remaining capital would, of course, have resulted in an equally substantial pro rata reduction in income. On the other hand, an increase in the size of the village would have increased the running costs. The fact that in mid-1921 the Trustees had thought it prudent to arrange an overdraft facility of up to £20,000 to be drawn upon if necessary to finance the building work then in hand, rather than deplete their remaining capital reserves, is a good indication of the financial situation which they faced. This overdraft facility was never used because in the event the surplus of income being generated over expenditure proved sufficient to meet the costs as they were incurred. For the future, however, the Trustees would feel it necessary to accumulate a sufficient surplus from income to be sure of being able to fund new projects before embarking upon them.

It was therefore not until 1923 that any plans for further buildings were prepared. The first requirement then was to extend the rest home, and Sir Aston Webb was commissioned to draw up the plans for this work which it was proposed should be carried out the following year. Henry Martin Ltd. were again awarded the contract at a price of £17,850 and work duly began early in 1924.

The Trustees also decided to build a laundry for the village to be situated behind Pondhead Cottage, as well as a Nonconformist chapel and a chaplain's house; the Revd Pouncey, who was still living in 17 Circle Road, had reminded them that he had been promised this when he had accepted his appointment in 1920. The site selected for the chaplaincy was on the west side of the North Avenue, next to St Mark's. Four possible sites were considered for the Nonconformist chapel: at the end of Hornbeam Walk; slightly to the south-east of the end of Hornbeam Walk; at the end of Heather Walk; and on the south side of Octagon Road, east of the junction with South Avenue.

The last of these alternative sites was chosen in June 1924, and the plans for this chapel and for the laundry and chaplaincy were drawn up during the second half of 1924. In December of that year, the contract for their construction, amounting to £14,063 for all three buildings, was placed with Henry Martin Ltd. Work started early the next year, and proceeded simultaneously with the work to extend the rest home, which was still going on. It had been decided to call the new Nonconformist chapel The Sanctuary and the foundation stone for this was laid on 30 April 1925 by Colonel the Hon A. G. Brodrick, TD, DL, the Chairman of the Trustees' Executive Committee. All these building works were completed in late 1925 or the first half of 1926, and The Sanctuary was officially opened for worship at a service held there on Thursday, 20 May 1926 conducted by the Minister, Revd J. E. Flower, and attended by Colonel Brodrick and Mr W. E. Gillett.

These projects having been completed and paid for, the possible extension of the village was again discussed in July 1926 and approved in principle, although once again the Trustees found themselves obliged to defer the start of any new building work, until they had accumulated a sufficient sum to pay for it from the surplus of income remaining from the Trust's investment income, after the expenses of running the village had been met. To make matters worse, building costs had risen steeply over the previous few years, with the result that new single cottages which had cost £400 to £500 each in the original contract would now cost almost double that.

When considering how best to extend the village, the Trustees, for reasons which are not explained, appear not to have taken any further account of Mr Atkinson's original plan for the village (see Appendix H: Plan W) which had provided for

43. Interior view of the Sanctuary.

considerably more cottages than had actually been built. Instead, they asked Sir Aston Webb to plan the proposed extension. His plan, dated March 1927, envisaged the eventual construction of an additional 179 cottages, of which 141 were to be single and the remaining 38 double, thus providing accommodation for another 217 villagers. Having been decided by the Trustees that the area within Circle Road surrounding the monument should be kept as an open space, Sir Aston Webb's plan was for all the new cottages to be built outside the Octagon in seven groups; those at the ends of Chestnut, Heather and Hornbeam Walks to be laid out as Crescents, and those at the ends of North, South, East and West Avenues to be laid out as Squares. The proposed new cottages were all to be of a similar size and construction to those already built.

Work on the first extension, Chestnut Crescent, was begun in the summer of 1928, the contract having again been placed with Henry Martin Ltd., who had submitted a tender of £12,791 for the construction of the 12 single and four double cottages to be built there – an average price of almost £800 per cottage. These cottages were completed in June 1929. On each side of the Crescent, the two central blocks of cottages were joined by an arch. Over the arch facing south-east, the date (1929) was inscribed together with the words 'Rest and be Thankful', which were chosen by the Bishop of London; over the north-west facing arch a sundial was erected. These were the last cottages to be built in the village.

As will be seen from the map dated 1919 in Appendix K, the Trust estate did not at that time include the 25-acre plot of land in the north-west corner, bounded by

Seven Hills Road on the west and by Burwood Road on the north. From about 1920 onwards the Trustees became interested in acquiring this plot, which they felt would 'round off' the estate nicely. It belonged to the Walton Poor's Land Trustees, and was especially designated for use as allotments. On being approached, its trustees replied that they would be perfectly willing to exchange the plot for another site or sites in the area of equivalent value, but made it clear that they had no funds with which to pay the costs which would be incurred in such a transaction. The Whiteley Homes Trustees had many other financial commitments at that time, and so the matter rested there until September 1927, when it was discovered that Walton Urban District Council was interested in acquiring the plot to use as a cemetery.

The Trustees quickly decided that they did not really want a cemetery adjoining the village and re-opened negotiations with the Walton Poor's Land Trustees, who were fortunately still willing to negotiate a suitable exchange. Direct purchase had been ruled out on the grounds that it might set a precedent which would one day result in them having divested themselves of all the land they held for use as allotments. In order to effect the exchange, the Whiteley Homes Trustees acquired four small 'parcels' of local land, viz:

Description	Owner	Acreage	Price
Part of Home Farm, Walton	T. W. Ashley	12.851	£1,230
Land in Rydens Road	W. Stoneham	14.146	£1,839
Land adjoining Burhill Road	Burhill Estates Co. Ltd.	13.548	£1,500
Land near Walton Grove	Executors of Mr Cababe	12.491	£1,000
Total		53.036	£5,569

The land at the corner of the Trust's estate was valued at £5,125 and so, in order to reconcile the values, a reduction in the size (and therefore the value) of the plot purchased in Ryden's Road was made.

The formal exchange, which was subject to the agreement of both the Ministry of Agriculture (responsible for seeing that the acreage available as allotments was maintained) and the Charity Commissioners, was not completed until 1929, when the plot became part of Whiteley Park. As a result, the council had to look elsewhere for a suitable site for a cemetery, and eventually acquired the land adjoining Burvale Road on which Burvale Cemetery is now situated.

For financial reasons having found themselves unable to proceed any further with their proposed extension of the village after the completion of the cottages in

Chestnut Crescent (which had become known as 'J' section), the Trustees nevertheless decided, in October 1929, to build an extension to the village club to provide a library at a cost of £1,150. This was again carried out by Henry Martin Ltd., who had constructed the original building. Later, in January 1932, they decided to extend further the home of rest by enlarging the kitchen and dining facilities and by building on a nurses' home, thus releasing the accommodation previously occupied by nurses within the home of rest itself for use by villagers. Work on this extension, which was yet again carried out by Henry Martin Ltd., began in September 1932 and was not completed until October 1934 at a final cost of just under £21,000.

By 1935 it had become apparent that there was really no longer a need for a London office and that a cost saving could be effected by consolidating all the Trust's activities at Whiteley Village. At a meeting held on 20 March that year the Trustees decided to:

Close the Trust office in London and move it to Whiteley Village as soon as possible.

Retire Mr Ingram, whose health was failing, on 30 June 1935 with a pension of £600 p.a. in recognition of over 25 years' devoted service to the Trust.

Appoint Mrs Cunningham, who had been acting as Mr Ingram's assistant since the end of the war, as his successor at a salary of £400 p.a. plus a cottage in the village when the office moved there.

By mid-1936 the Trustees had accumulated sufficient funds to begin contemplating some new building work, and the possibility of starting on Hornbeam Crescent, in accordance with Sir Aston Webb's plan, was discussed. The Trustees also considered extending Fox Oak to accommodate the staff who would need to move to the village when the London office closed, but abandoned this idea in favour of building a new office block on the south-west corner of the junction of Octagon Road and West Avenue. This new block was designed to provide an office each for the general manager (as he was still known), the Lady Warden and the Secretary (who would be moving from London), together with smaller offices for their clerks, a strong room, a waiting-room that could double as a pay office, and a boardroom. Care was taken to ensure that the design of the building fitted in with the villagers' cottages nearby and with the model cottages on the opposite corner. A decision then had to be made as to whether to proceed with Hornbeam Crescent or with the new office block, as the finance available was insufficient for both. The office block was considered the more urgent in view of the savings that would accrue when the London office was shut, and was therefore proceeded with instead of Hornbeam Crescent. There was, however, sufficient surplus money to build an extra pair of matching staff houses in Combe Lane, bringing the total there to eight.

44.   The new office block.

Miss Gabbett's communal kitchen, which had originally been intended as no more than a temporary measure to help villagers overcome the food shortages that had become quite serious by the end of 1917, flourished throughout this period. The kitchen had been established in the room on the right of the entrance to the village stores (where the bowls clubroom is now) and each villager was provided with a 'meal carrier' in the form of a long metal can divided into three sections; the bottom section being for vegetables, the middle section for meat and the top section for pudding. The routine was that those villagers who wanted their midday meal from the kitchen would bring their meal carriers to the stores waiting-room (the room on the left of the entrance to the village stores, where the library is now) during the course of the morning, and then collect their filled cans at about noon. In 1920 each meal cost 6d. – 4d. for the meat and vegetables and 2d. for the pudding. By 1939, the price had only increased to 8d. The kitchen was obviously very well-patronised by the villagers, so the standard of the food provided was undoubtedly good despite the low price. Every villager received two free meal tickets per week, and could obtain more if they did not take their full ration of free coal. Bridget Nolan, a notable village character, remained as the chief cook throughout this period.

During the winter months, each villager received a free delivery of one hundredweight of coal per week, providing that they were at home when the delivery cart got to their cottage! In the summer, from May to August inclusive, this amount was reduced to one hundredweight per fortnight, and villagers who had sufficient to meet their needs could decline the coal and receive additional meal tickets instead, as explained in the following notice:

W. V.

Coal Notice

Coal will be distributed next week (May 19th & 21st) as usual.

    Afterwards the distribution will be fortnightly during the summer months, to those Villagers who are at home at the time of delivery.

    During the months of May, June, July and August, Villagers who have a store of coal in their Cottages sufficient for an emergency, such as illness, may exercise the option of declining coal, and receive food tickets at their Sectional Pay Day in the following week instead.

               H.E. Cooke,
           Agent & General Manager.

May 14th, 1925.

After the winter, of course, the chimneys needed sweeping, and the next notice describes the arrangement for this to be done:

W. V.

N O T I C E

Beginning on Monday next May 11th, chimneys will be swept in strict rotation, beginning at Section A and going on in numerical order.

    No request for postponement can be entertained.

    It must be clearly understood that Villagers who decline the services of the Chimney Sweep when proffered, must make their own arrangements at their own expense.

               H.E. Cooke,
           Agent & General Manager.

5th May, 1936.

During this period, the Trustees imposed quite a considerable measure of control over the daily routine of the villagers. The 'Lighting Order' is a case in point. As has already been noted in chapter five, this required villagers to turn their lights out at 10 p.m. and prohibited them from turning them on again until 6.30 a.m. A night-watchman was employed whose duty it was to go round and check that this order was being obeyed. The rationale for this Order was undoubtedly the fact that the Trust was paying for all the electricity consumed, as the notice below indicates:

> ### N O T I C E.
> ### E L E C T R I C   L I G H T.
>
> The consumption of electricity is increasing unreasonably.
> Villagers are specially requested not to waste light:-
>
> (1) By leaving light burning when they are not at home.
>
> (2) By burning lights in the living room and other rooms
>   at the same time.
>
> (3) By forgetting to turn off the light when it is no
>   longer needed.
>
> Remember we are on our honour not to waste light which is
> generously given to us, but which costs a lot of money.
>
>   H. B. COOKE,
> 27 January, 1930.   Agent & General Manager.

Specific extensions of the permitted hours were granted at Christmas and on other special occasions. By 1936, pressure had obviously mounted for a more general relaxation of the Order which, although granted, was still far from generous as far as the villagers were concerned:

> Stations:
> WALTON OR WEYBRIDGE   WHITELEY VILLAGE,
>   SOUTHERN RAIL,
>   2 MILES   WALTON-ON-THAMES
>   Telephone:
> 360 WEYBRIDGE.
>
>   28th November, 1936
>
> ELECTRIC   LIGHT
>
>   The Trustees have kindly decided that in
> future no time shall be fixed for
> extinguishing lights in houses occupied by
> members of the staff.
>
>   G. S. CHETWYND-STAPYLTON.
>   Agent & General Manager.

Stations:
WALTON ON WEYBRIDGE
SOUTHERN RLY.
2 MILES
Telephone:
360 WEYBRIDGE.

WHITELEY VILLAGE,
WALTON-ON-THAM

30th November, 1936

ELECTRIC LIGHT

The Trustees have kindly consented to allow
lights in the cottages to be kept on until
10 30 p.m. if required. It is hoped that those
who avail themselves of this concession will be
careful not to cause inconvenience to any of their
neighbours who may wish to retire earlier.

G. B. CHETWYND STAPYLTON.
Agent & General Manager.

From the start it had been recognised that the village was somewhat isolated and that the residents would have to be provided with transport to enable them to come and go freely. By as early as 1920 there was a regular bus service running between the village and Walton-on-Thames, at a fare of 2d. for villagers and 6d. for non-villagers. To make sure of getting a seat it was necessary to book it in advance by writing one's name in a reservation book kept at the entrance to the village stores, which was the starting point. Those who had not put their names in the book had to wait and see if there were any seats left vacant after all those who had booked had got on board. So two queues would often form on opposite sides of the entrance, one consisting of those who had booked and the other of those who had not. These two groups became known as 'the sheep' and 'the goats'! Sometimes the regular service was suspended so that the bus could be used for special outings or for another special purpose, as described in the notice:

HERAM DISTRICT COUNCIL ELECTION

In the hope that all who have votes for the election
of our Representatives for three years on the District
Council will exercise their privilege, the Trustees
have decided to convey Village Voters to the Poll at
Hersham on Saturday April 4th in the Motor Omnibus.

Leaving Stores at

2 p.m.

2.30

3.0

3.30

4.0

6.0 (for Staff)

Names should be put down at the Village Stores before
noon on Saturday. There will be no charge.

H.E. Cooke,
Agent & General Manager.

3rd, April, 1925.

The omnibus referred to in Chapter Five was replaced in late 1929 by a large 'Dennis' coach, and this, in turn, was replaced by a 'Morris' coach in 1933. The village was at this time in practice running a public bus service – a fact which, in May 1934, attracted the attention of the London Passenger Transport Board who wrote to the Trustees telling them that, in order to comply with the regulations governing the provision of such a service, they required their formal permission together with a licence from the Metropolitan Traffic Commissioner. The Trustees did not answer this letter but told Mr Cooke, the agent, to '... see the Parliamentary Officer of the London Passenger Transport Board' if they persisted in their claim. Nothing further was heard until the following year when the driver, Mr Coote, was told by a passenger who had boarded the bus in the village that he was an inspector from the Transport Board. He took Mr Coote's name and address. Two months later when Mr Cooke (the agent and general manager) and Mr Coote (the driver) were both served with summonses for using a motor vehicle as a stage carriage without a licence, each was fined 2s. 6d. Acting on legal advice, the Trustees stopped charging a fare for travelling on the village bus, with the result that the number of passengers increased considerably. The village bus service remains free to this day.

From the beginning the Trustees had taken care to ensure that the grounds were well-kept and attractively laid out. This included encouraging villagers to keep the small plots in front of their cottages in good order. Manure was made available (at a price) and advice given on the use of lime, as the next two notices show. Occasionally it was thought necessary to issue a warning such as that contained in the third notice.

```
              N O T I C E.


A limited quantity of manure can be spared,

and Villagers and Members of the Staff with

gardens or allotments can purchase one cwt.

each, for one shilling delivered, by filling

up an application form with prepayment at

the Village Stores at any time before (but

not after) Saturday March 6th next.




                    H. K. COOKE.


                    Agent & General Manager,
```

8th February, 1932.

N O T I C E .

LIME AS A GARDEN DRESSING.

Lime is not in itself a manure, but a solvent. It frees the nitrates in the ground, and makes them available for plant life.   Our soil, like all the Bagshot Sand, is very deficient in Lime, and an occasional dressing is very beneficial as a stimulant.

A limited quantity of agricultural lime is now on sale at the Village Stores, where a paper bag containing about 12 lbs weight can be bought for three pence. This is ample for a small garden.   The lime should be applied at once,- lightly forked in and kept clear from the roots.   Please note that lime is injurious to rhododendrons.

H. E. COOKE,

Agent & General Manager.

W. V.

NOTICE.

In order that all may enjoy the beauty of the flowers, Villagers and members of the Staff are particularly requested not to pick or uproot the flowers, either wild or cultivated, growing in the Village or the woods.

H.E. Cooke,

Agent & General Manager.

April 29th, 1925.

It was also the policy of the Trustees, from the earliest days, to allow Scouts and Guides to camp in the village, as the following programme for Whitsun 1933 illustrates:

W H I T S U N   C A M P S.   1933.

1st Regents Park Co Girl Guides Ranger Camp May 31 - June 6 abou

   Captain. Miss Phyllis J. Gerson, 28 Christchurch Avenue,
                                     Brondesbury. N.W.

Surrey Guiders, 50. Miss Dorothy L. Taylor,
                Bellefielde, Englefield Green. June

St John the Divine Boy Scouts (about 10) in South Avenue
   (Mr A Butcher, Assistant Scoutmaster) June 3 to June 5.

W H I T E L E Y   V I L L A G E   H A L L.

The following Cinema Programme will be shown on Mondays at 6.30 p.m.
and on Tuesdays at 2.30 p.m. from Nov.30th to Feb. 1st, 1926.

P R O G R A M M E.

Nov.30 & Dec 1st.	Feature Interest Serial No.1		Butterfly Love Climbing the Strathhorn Vindicta
Dec 7 & 8.	Feature Interest Serial No.2		Women men Marry Italian Lakes Vindicta
Dec. 14 & 15	Feature Interest Serial No.3		Race with Death Chamonix Vindicta
Dec. 21 & 22	Feature Interest Serial No.4		Payment in Full Ascent to Rathorn Vindicta
Dec.28.& 29	Feature Interest Serial No.5		Spanish Passion Berne Vindicta
1926			
Jan.4 & 5	Feature Interest Serial No. 6		Angel Factory Rugged Wales Vindicta
Jan.11 & 12	Feature Interest Serial No. 7		Station Content Beauty Spots in Mediterranean Vindicta
Jan.18 & 19	Feature Interest Serial No.8		Vengeance of Durek Bath the Famous Spa Vindicta
Jan.25 & 26	Feature Interest Serial No.9		Riders of the Law Sky Trails Vindicta
Feb 1 & 2	Feature Interest Serial No.10		Shifting Sands Down the Strand Vindicta.

Regular use was made of the village hall as a place of entertainment, particularly during the winter months. There was some sort of show or play every Saturday evening at 8 p.m., and then on Monday evenings a cinema programme was screened. This was repeated on the Tuesday afternoon.

The films in this programme were, of course, all silent and it was not until 1934 that 'talkies' were screened:

```
Stations:                              WHITELEY VILLAGE,
WALTON OR WEYBRIDGE
  SOUTHERN RAIL.                        WALTON-ON-THAMES
    2 MILES
  Telephone:
360 WEYBRIDGE.                          14th April 1934.


              C I N E M A.


  The Trustees have decided to install Talking Picture

  Equipment in the Village Hall, and a special exhibition

  will be given on Monday evening next at 6.30 p.m., when

  the following programme will be given:-


       " Jack's the Boy "    ...    Jack Hulbert

       " One good turn "     ...    Laurel & Hardy

       " Flowers & Trees"    ...    Coloured Symphony
                                    (Walt. Disney)


                            H. E. COOKE,
                              Agent & General Manager.
```

Community singing was another popular form of entertainment in the hall, as the next two notices show:

```
Stations:                              WHITELEY VILLAGE.
WALTON OR WEYBRIDGE
  SOUTHERN RAIL.                        WALTON-ON-THAMES
    2 MILES
  Telephone:
360 WEYBRIDGE.
                            10th October, 1933.


              N O T I C E.
       C O M M U N I T Y    S I N G I N G.


  The Winter Session will begin on Tuesday next, October 17th

  and each subsequent Tuesday, meeting in the Village Hall at

  6.30 p.m.

        Conductor, Mr Barnes.        Accompanist,   Miss Coe


  All Residents in Whiteley Village, including new Villagers,

  are cordially invited to come.

  Subscription Nil.

                            H. E. Cooke,
                            Agent & General Manager
                            the Whiteley Homes Trust
```

```
Stations:                              WHITELEY VILLAGE,
WALTON OR WEYBRIDGE
   SOUTHERN RAIL.                           WALTON-ON-THAMES
     2 MILES
  Telephone:
360 WEYBRIDGE.                         30th April 1934.


              N O T I C E.


The last Community Singing for the season will be held in

the Village Hall on Tuesday evening May 1st. at 6.30 p.m.,

interspersed with solos and recitations.

      All are cordially invited.


                        H. E. COOKE,
                        Agent & General Manager
```

Also during the winter months a workshop was provided in the works yard:

```
                                    November 19th 1925.

           A R T S   &   C R A F T S.
           ─────────────────────────
              N O T I C E.


The Trustees have re-opened the Village Workshop in

which during the winter months any men in the Village

will be welcome to work at carpentering, picture framing,

furniture making and repairing, or any other hobby of

this nature.

      A Carpenter & Joiner will be in attendance, and

will give free advice and instruction, if desired, to

any who wish for help.

      Tools will be lent free for use in the Workshop.

Materials can be bought at cost price.

      The Workshop is situated at Minor Buildings in

Chestnut Avenue, - the first on the right hand side

behind the Electrical Station.  The hours will be

from 2 to 4.30 p.m. from Monday to Friday inclusive,

beginning next Monday, November 23rd.


                        H. E. Cooke.

                  Agent & General Manager,
                  for the Whiteley Homes Trustees.
```

During the summer months, excursions to local places of interest such as Hampton Court, Kew Gardens, Windsor and Guildford were arranged once a fortnight using the village bus. The church choir also had an annual outing. The bowls club had become active and in 1926 had their photograph taken.

```
                    Short   Notice.
                    _____

    If possible I am trying to get a Photographer
    this afternoon to take a photograph of members
    of the Whiteley Village Bowling Club on the
    old Bowling Green at 3 o'clock.

           Will members, whether playing in the
    match or not, who wish to be included in the
    group, assemble there at that time .

                         H.E. Cooke,
                    Agent & General Manager.
    26 August, 1936.
```

Apparently there were also those who wanted to do no more than sit and watch the traffic go by along Seven Hills Road:

```
                     "THE  DECK"
    The Trustees have caused a new sitting-out place,
    called "The Deck", to be constructed in the wood
    overlooking the Seven Hills Road with seats from
    which the traffic can be seen in safety.

           It is now ready for use by the Villagers
    and Staff, but is not intended for children unless
    accompanied by their Parents.


                         H.E. Cooke,
                    Agent & General Manager.
    20 June, 1928.
```

The remains of 'The Deck' can still be seen just inside the fence to the north of West Lodge.

A major annual event was the Trustees' garden party, held in June each year. The notice reproduced below gives the details for the 1933 event and is followed by a copy of one of the invitation cards issued.

This garden party usually included some sort of show or play put on by the villagers, and after the workshop had been set up, began to include a display of villagers' work:

45.   The Village Show, 1925: watching the play.

A R T S   &   C R A F T S.

    On the day of the Trustees' Garden Party July 6th it is
intended to exhibit in the Games Room of the Village Club
the work of the Villagers in the Workshop during the past
season.

    Those who have availed themselves of the Workshop
are asked to be kind enough to lend their handiwork, and a
Van will call on Friday July 5th in the morning.

H. S. COOKE,

Agent & General Manage

1st July, 1929

46.   The Village Show, 1925: spectators (Bishop Winnington-Ingram in the centre).

ARMISTICE SUNDAY 8th NOVEMBER, 1931.

As in 1930, and with the concurrence of the Chaplain,
there will be a Village Church Parade to St. Mark's Church,
organised by Mr. Messenger, on Sunday 8th November, leaving
the Monument at 10.45 a.m. punctually.

All Ex-Service men and women in the Village, both
members of the Staff and Villagers, are cordially invited
to fall in at the Monument not later than 10.40 a.m.

5th November, 1931.   H. B. Cooke,
                                          Agent & General Manager

St George's Day seems also to have been celebrated, as the following slightly oddly-worded notice shows:

```
                                            APRIL 25rd, 1929.


TO-DAY, APRIL 23rd, IS ST. GEORGE'S DAY, ENGLAND'S DAY,

ZEEBRUGGE DAY, AND SHAKESPEARE DAY.    THAT IS WHY THE

FLAGS ARE FLYING.

                                    H. E. C.
```

Christmas each year was marked by a gift to each villager, by the Trustees, of some Christmas fare:

```
                    CHRISTMAS, 1926.
                    ─────────────────

The Trustees have kindly arranged to give Christmas fare
to each Villager on Christmas Eve next.
An alternative bill of fare is offered, either from the
Kitchen or the Stores as set out below, and in order that
the Lady Warden may be able to make the necessary preparations
each Villager is asked to decide which alternative is
preferred, and to tell the Pay Clerk their decision on
Section Pay day during the week ending 27th November.
                    Either
        Kitchen     Portion of Turkey and ham with potatoes
                    and sprouts;  Plum pudding, mince pie,
                    and custard;  box of dates.
                        Or
        Stores      A tin of biscuits, and a tin of tea.
Please remember that the choice when made cannot be altered.
            The arrangements for the Trustees' Tea to
Villagers and Staff after Christmas will be announced later on.
                    H.E. Cooke,
                    Agent & General Manager.

17th November, 1926.
```

A Christmas tea was also held to which members of staff as well as villagers were invited:

```
Stations:
WALTON ON WEYBRIDGE.                        WHITELEY VILLAGE,
  L. & S. W. R'LY.
    & W.H.S.                                  WALTON-ON-THAMES.
Telephone:
  660 WEYBRIDGE.                          December 28th 1925.


              NOTICE.

         A cordial invitation is extended to the Estate
     Workmen to attend the Trustees' Christmas Tea and
     Tree in the Village Hall at 3 o'clock on Wednesday
     next, 30th December.
         Married men are asked to bring their wives with
     them.
         Work will cease at 12.30 p.m. but time will
     be paid until 5 o'clock as usual to all those who
     are working on that morning.

                              H. E. Cooke.

                         Agent & General Manager.
```

On Founder's Day, in accordance with the wish expressed in his will (see Appendix A, para 39[5]) a birthday present of 10s. (50p) was given to each villager:

```
                    W. V.
               Founder's Birthday.
          ────────────────────────

     In honour of the Founder's Birthday which falls on
     Michaelmas Day, 29th September, the Trustees have
     decided to give a birthday present of ten shillings
     to each Villager.

              Distribution will begin on Monday next,
     September 21st, and I hope to call at each house as
     far as possible, beginning at 2 p.m. in the several
     Sections as follow:-

              Section A    Mon.   Sept.  21
                 "     B    Tues.   "     22
                 "     C    Wed.    "     23
                 "     D    Thurs.  "     24
                 "     E    Fri.    "     25
                 "     F    Mon.    "     28
                 "     G    Tues.   "     29
                 "     H    Wed.    "     30.

                              H.E. Cooke

     15 Sept. 1925.        Agent & General Manager.
```

Special events were celebrated in an appropriate manner, as was, for example, the Royal Silver Jubilee of 1935:

Stations:
TON OR WEYBRIDGE
SOUTHERN RAIL.
3 MILES
Telephone:
360 WEYBRIDGE.

WHITELEY VILLAGE.

WALTON-ON-THAMES

N O T I C E S.

2nd May, 1935.

ROYAL   SILVER   JUBILEE.

Monday next, May 6th, being the 25th anniversary of Their Majesties' Accession to the Throne, will be observed as a public holiday.

The Village Stores and Kitchen will be closed on Monday, and the only Omnibus service will be as follows :-

Village Stores dep. 7. 20 a.m. in connexion with the up train due at Walton at 7. 43 a.m. for Waterloo.
Names must be put down at the Stores before 5. p.m. on Saturday.

Walton Station dep. 11. 0. p.m. in connexion with the down train due at Walton at 10. 58. (Waterloo 10. 20)

Owing to pressure of traffic, train services may be late and crowded.
On Monday next the gate at North Lodge will be kept unlocked until 11. 30 p.m. in order to admit any residents who may wish to watch the Jubilee Bonfires, which are timed to be lit at 10. p.m. The Lighting Order will be extended until midnight.

Our own Village celebrations will take place on the following Saturday, May 11th, when the under-mentioned programme has been kindly arranged by the Trustees:-

7. p.m.   High Tea in the Village Clubhouse.
8. p.m.   Concert & Entertainment in the Village Hall
            by Mrs Eyre, Mr Bontoux and others. .
10 to)   Illumination of the Monument, best seen from
10 15)   the Terrace outside the Hall, and fireworks.

To these three functions the Trustees extend invitations to:-
Villagers, Members of the Staff and their Families, the Choir Girls, and the Sunday School Children.

Owing to the numbers expected. it is regretted that no other guests can be invited. The Lighting Order on Saturday May 11th will be extended until 11 p.m.

H. E. COOKE,

Agent & General Manager.

In the early days, the routine in the house of rest was very strict, and residents were woken at 5 a.m. with a cup of tea! In addition, visitors were restricted to the afternoons between 2 p.m. and 6 p.m., and, for the hospital, to Sunday afternoons only. Other rules or 'requests' were that there should be:

No baths taken after 7 p.m.

No talking in the corridors (so as not to disturb other residents).

Forty-eight hours' notice given for leave of absence, supported by permission from the doctor.

In 1934, these rules were considerably relaxed, as the copy of the 'Information Card' in Appendix Q shows.

The way in which villagers cared for their cottages attracted occasional criticism, as the following notice illustrates:

Sanitary Notice.

The Trustees have received a report on the recent inspection of fixtures and fittings entrusted by them to the care of Villagers, and although in the majority of cottages the report is good there are still some cases of neglect.

I am especially instructed to call the attention of Villagers, who have already been warned, to the necessity of keeping their gas stoves, baths, W.C.pans, and sinks scrupulously clean. It is for example very insanitary and very injurious to a gas stove to allow drippings of water or fat to lie uncleaned and to corrode and rust the ironwork. Baths must be kept free from stores of any kind, and sinks and W.C. pans cleansed and brushed daily.

The matter is so important that if this notice is not regarded by those whom it concerns I am to say that individual action will be taken by the Trustees.

H .E. Cooke,

Agent & General Manager.

17 Dec. 1925.

Frost precautions in winter were also a matter of concern:

F R O S T.

To prevent frost-bits and the misery of after-flooding,

Villagers and members of the Staff are earnestly requested:-

(1) To keep scullery and lavatory windows closed during
     severe frost.

(2) Not to leave taps running (a dangerous practice)

(3) To give notice at once in all cases where pipes are frozen
     or taps refuse to flow .

12th February 1932.   H.E.Cooke,

                              Agent & General Manager.

On a different note, thought was also being given to the provision for villagers of useful services:

                                    31st October, 1929.
              N O T I C E.

INSURANCE AGAINST BURGLARY, HOUSEBREAKING AND LARCENY.
————————————————————————————————————

     Inquiries having been made by Villagers, the Trustees have
made provisional arrangements with the Commercial Union
Assurance Co Ltd. for special terms for this class of insurance
on a schedule basis, which after giving Villagers the benefit of
the agency commission works out at:-

     1s 8d annual premium for £100 insurance

        10d   "   "   "   £50   "

upon the understanding that the amount insured in any one name
represents the total value of such property, and that the value
of gold and silver articles, jewellery & furs does not exceed
one-third of the individual totals.

     Villagers or members of the staff who would like to avail
themselves of the terms offered by the Commercial Union Office
can let us know. No money to be sent at present.

                              H. E. COOKE.

                         Agent & General Manager.

Leave of Absence, however, was obviously strictly controlled:

```
Stations:
WALTON ON WEYBRIDGE                        WHITELEY VILLAGE,
   SOUTHERN RAIL.
     & MILES                                   WALTON-ON-THAMES
Telephone:
860 WEYBRIDGE.
                                          18th February, 1938


            A B S E N C E.

    Villagers are reminded that no absence should extend
beyond one calendar month in either half-year (January to
June or July to December) Those therefore, who expect
invitations to stay away at Christmas, should not be so
lavish with their Summer holiday, that Christmas finds
them with none of their second half-year's leave in hand.

                           G. B. Chetwynd-Stapylton,
                               Warden.
```

Then, in 1936, television arrived:

```
                        W. V.
                  N O T I C E.
                  ―――――――――――――

Television Demonstration at Messrs Rogers & Sons.


The first 31 names on the list will be taken by bus
from the Village Stores at 2.15 p.m. on Monday December 7th.
The remainder (up to a total of 31) will be taken on
Monday 14th inst. at the same time.

                           G. B. Chetwynd-Stapylton.
5th December 1936.              Warden
```

It is not known how much trade Messrs Rogers and Sons got from the village at that time; probably not much, for the sets were then very expensive.

The period covered by this chapter was basically one of peace. It should not be forgotten that there was still no social security system as we know it today, and that, although the Trustees imposed what would now be regarded as a very strict regime on the villagers, they were undoubtedly well cared for. Some recollections of what life in the village was like at that time are given in Appendix R.

By the end of this period the country was once again facing the prospect of war. In April 1938 the Trustees gave permission for the village bus to be used to take members of staff into Walton and Weybridge for lectures on air raid precautions. The outbreak of the Second World War was then less than 18 months away.

Chapter Eight

THE SECOND WORLD WAR AND ITS AFTERMATH (1938-47)

By the middle of 1938 it had become clear that war with Nazi Germany could not be avoided for long, and preparations for the inevitable had begun, both nationally and locally. As early as September of that year arrangements were being made to issue the population with gas-masks, for which they had, of course, to be measured:

> September 22nd 1938.
>
> A I R   R A I D   P R E C A U T I O N S.
>
> To ensure that in a state of emergency each person will
> be issued with a gas mask of the right size, qualified members
> of the Staff will, shortly be visiting Sections to take
> measurements.
>
> G.B.Chetwynd-Stapylton
>
> Warden.

These were issued before the end of the year. Thought was also being given to the need for Air Raid Precautions, as the following notice shows:

> A I R   R A I D   P R E C A U T I O N S
>
> It might be a wise precaution to lay in the following:-
>
> (1)   Sufficient cellophane paper, or other suitable material,
>   to paste over the windows to prevent splintering.
>   (See Home Office Pamphlet "The Protection of your
>   Home against Air Raids" page 16)
>   This material can be purchased at Woolworths or Timothy
>   Whites, or can be gradually saved from wrappings.
>
> (2)   A supply of candles, matches or serviceable electric
>   torches.
>
> (3)   A little tinned food.
>
> (4)   Material for darkening windows.
>
> (5)   Bags of any material (measuring about 33 inches by 14 inches
>   preferably) open at one end, which could be used as
>   sandbags.

Early in 1939, several members of staff volunteered for National Service with the Territorial Army or the Red Cross, and the Trustees readily agreed to allow the men paid leave for the two-week period of their TA training and to make the women a special allowance towards the cost of their Red Cross uniforms. They also decided that, should any of them be posted away, their accommodation in the village would be kept for them.

In the village, an experimental air-raid shelter to hold 48 people was built in F Section under the direction of Colonel Gillett. Although not gas-proof (there was a very real concern at this time that the Germans would make substantial and indiscriminate use of poison gas against the civilian population), this shelter was considered to be 'reasonably blast-proof and splinter-proof'. It was, in fact, an extremely rugged reinforced-concrete construction, of which about two-thirds was below the surface of the ground in order to give extra protection. The plans for it are in Appendix S. By the outbreak of war, a sufficient number of these shelters had been built to hold all the residents of the village in the event of an air raid. These shelters, although crude, really were extremely strong, and would undoubtedly have protected the occupants against almost anything other than a direct hit.

By April of 1939, most villagers were preparing to 'blackout' their windows at night; indeed the Warden obviously felt that some were being over-enthusiastic:

WALTON ON WEYBRIDGE.
SOUTHERN RAIL.
2 MILES
Telephone:
360 WEYBRIDGE

WHITELEY VILLAGE,
WALTON-ON-THAMES.

19th April, 1939

A I R   R A I D   P R E C A U T I O N S

Villagers are not asked to buy a lot of expensive material for darkening windows; those, however, who do make special curtains will be helped in fixing them.   Otherwise what is required is some material at hand, even thick brown paper, which could be fixed in a hurry if the Authorities order a complete "black out".

G. B. Chetwynd-Stapylton,
Warden.

Fire practices were also being held at which training in using the fire-fighting equipment was given:

Stations:
WALTON ON WEYBRIDGE
SOUTHERN RAIL.
2 MILES
Telephone:
360 WEYBRIDGE.

WHITELEY VILLAGE,
WALTON-ON-THAMES

21st. April, 1939

F I R E   B R I G A D E.

The usual allowance will be made for the next practice but, after that, members are asked to attend sufficiently often without renumeration to become throughly efficient in handling the new gear.

G. B. Chetwynd-Stapylton,
Warden.

Then, in early July 1939, a 'black-out' exercise was held:

```
WALTON ON WEYBRIDGE                              WHITELEY VILLAGE,
    SOUTHERN RAIL.
      8 MILES                                       WALTON-ON-THAMES
   Telephone :
 560 WEYBRIDGE.                                       7th July 1939

       A I R    R A I D    P R E C A U T I O N S

       NIGHT    OF    SATURDAY   8th    JULY   1939

    To assist the Royal Air Force "Black-out" exercise this

    week-end it is requested that the utmost care be taken
                                      Completely
    that all lights remain extinguished or carefully screened

    from view from outside between 12 midnight on Saturday

    8th July until 4 a.m. on Sunday 9th instant.

                        G. B. Chetwynd-Stapylton,
                              Warden
```

(As all villagers were still supposed to put their lights out by not later than 10.30 p.m. there really should not have been any offenders!)

At this time too, an air-raid warning siren was erected on a scaffold behind the village club. In order to camouflage it as well as possible, the trees surrounding it were left in place and the scaffold was painted green.

Naturally, with all these preparations both nationally and in the village and with alarming news appearing regularly in the newspapers, some villagers became anxious. The Warden and staff did their best to reassure them, but the Warden nevertheless felt obliged to advise those going away on holiday to take their gas masks with them, adding a hopeful reassurance '... this does not imply that a crisis is considered imminent'. It was nevertheless rapidly approaching.

On 2 September, the day before war was officially declared, the Warden issued the following notices:

```
                                        2nd September, 1939

            L I G H T I N G    R E S T R I C T I O N S

    Lighting Restrictions are in force every day from sunset

to sunrise.   Villagers who have not yet had special curtain rods

fixed should put up their dark curtains on the existing rods.

    No light whatever must be visible from outside.   If the

light shows through the curtain a dark shade of brown paper or

other material must be placed over the shade on the side nearest

the window.
                              G. B. Chetwynd-Stapylton
                                   Warden
```

```
Stations:
WALTON OR WEYBRIDGE.              WHITELEY VILLAGE,
   SOUTHERN RAIL.
   2 MILES.                         WALTON-ON-THAMES.
  Telephone:
 360 WEYBRIDGE.
                                    2nd September, 1939

          A I R   R A I D S

     In the event of an air-raid Villagers in D and R and J
Sections, who do not wish to remain in their houses should go
to one of the Shelters nearest at hand.
     If the Siren is not working the "Action Warning" will be
given by a series of sharp blasts on a whistle.
                              G. B. Chetwynd-Stapylton
                                    Warden
```

When war was officially declared the following day, 3 September, nothing changed immediately; this was the period later to be called the 'phoney war'. Shortages were, however, beginning to make themselves felt, and the village bus service had to be radically curtailed due to petrol being severely rationed:

```
Stations:
WALTON OR WEYBRIDGE.              WHITELEY VILLAGE,
   SOUTHERN RAIL.
   2 MILES.                        WALTON-ON-THAMES.
  Telephone.
 360 WEYBRIDGE.                     2nd September, 1939

        VILLAGE OMNIBUS
     Beginning on 4th September and until further notice there
will only be two journeys daily into Walton, viz:-
     10 a.m. from Stores (as at present) and
     2 p.m. from Stores, leaving the Square at 3.15 p.m.  Taking
passengers for the 2.20 up-train on the outward journey and
meeting the 3.23 down-train on the return, except on Wednesday.
     On Wednesday the 2 p.m. bus will go to the Station only to
meet the 2.20 up-train and the 2.23 down-train.
                              G.B. Chetwynd-Stapylton
                                    Warden
```

Villagers were asked for help in completing the air-raid shelters:

```
          N O T I C E            5th September, 1939
     If any Villagers would like to do some earth-shovelling
on the Air Raid Shelters, Mr. Blakemore would be glad to allot
them tasks.
                              G. B. Chetwynd-Stapylton
                                    Warden
```

they were also asked to economise in their consumption of electricity by using 25W bulbs instead of 40W or 60W:

```
                                        September 19th 1939.
    LIGHTING    RESTRICTIONS.

    Any Villager wishing to exchange a 40 or 60 watt lamp for

a 25 watt lamp in order to help the "black-out" and to ECONOMISE

IN LIGHTING may apply to Mr Blakemore.
```

Others helped by painting kerbstones white so that they could be more easily seen in the blackout.

Several members of staff were called up for military service, among them Roy Page (son of the lorry driver, David Page), George King the chauffeur, and John Wallace. Young Roy Page went into the Royal Marines, where, as a corporal, he was awarded the Norwegian Cross in October 1942 and then later in March 1943, having been promoted to sergeant, the Distinguished Service Medal. King and Wallace were both posted to the Far East, where they were captured and died in Japanese prisoner-of-war camps.

Villagers were naturally keen to help the war effort. In September 1939 Miss Taylor (the Warden's assistant) organised the making of garments for the Red Cross and later for the Armed Forces. This proved popular and successful; from then until the war ended in 1945 Whiteley Village contributed more than 6,400 garments sending:

> 700 to the Royal Navy
> 1,500 to the Red Cross
> 3,905 to the Lord Lieutenant of Surrey's appeal

The cost of making these garments came to about £625 and was financed partly by the Trustees but predominantly by fund-raising events organised by the villagers themselves. Whist drives and sales raised £240, and a 'penny-a-week' box in the communal kitchen raised another £140.

Identity cards and ration books were issued to everyone. Some villagers needed help:

```
                                        25th May, 1940


            RATION    BOOKS


    Villagers requiring help in filling up applications for

new ration books may attend at the office on Monday or Tuesday

afternoon.    They should also bring their identity cards with them.



            G. B. Chetwynd-Stapylton,
                Warden.
```

As the war progressed into 1940, shortages became more acute. The traditional Trustees' garden party was first of all replanned as a simple tea with no guests, and then postponed:

5th April 1940

MESSAGE FROM THE TRUSTEES

Dear Villagers,

      The Trustees regret that, owing to the War, it will not be possible to hold the annual Garden Party this year, but they will be meeting at Whiteley Village on Saturday 22nd June, when they hope to have the pleasure of entertaining Villagers and resident members of the Staff to tea in the Village Hall at 3.15 p.m. (for 3.30 p.m.).

      They regret that they cannot include Villagers' friends and relations in their invitation this time owing to lack of room.

      The Trustees share your disappointment that entertainment on the usual scale is not possible but they look forward to greeting you all again and enjoying a happy afternoon with you.

      Yours sincerely,

      G. B. CHETWYND-STAPYLTON

Stations:
WALTON OR WEYBRIDGE
SOUTHERN RAIL.
3 MILES
Telephone:
360 WEYBRIDGE.

WHITELEY VILLAGE,

WALTON-ON-THAMES

June 4th 1940.

NOTICE.

      In view of the situation the Trustees think it advisable to postpone the Reception and Tea arranged for June 22nd, and it will therefore not take place on that date.   It is hoped, however, to hold it later on.

      G.B.Chetwynd - Stapylton

      Warden.

In fact, it was not held again until 1947.

Swill bins were set up round the village, firstly as an experiment, and then on a permanent basis:

4th May, 1940

NATIONAL ECONOMY

As an experiment a dust bin will be placed, on Monday, under the arch between North Avenue and A Section for the collection of Swill for the pigs. This will be cleared each morning before breakfast.

Residents of A Section are asked to place their Swill in the receptacle provided, but, NO SOAP
NO SODA
NO (TEA   PLEASE
(LEAVES

G. B. Chetwynd-Stapylton,
Warden

Stations:
WALTON OR WEYBRIDGE
SOUTHERN RAIL.
3 MILES
Telephone:
360 WEYBRIDGE.

WHITELEY VILLAGE,

WALTON-ON-THAMES

June 8th 1940.

NATIONAL   ECONOMY.

Dustbins for the collection of swill for the pigs will be now placed under the arches in D and F Sections as well as in A Section. These will be cleared daily before breakfast.

NO SOAP, NO SODA, NO TEA LEAVES OR FISH BONES PLEASE.

G.B.Chetwynd-Stapylton,

Warden.

ALUMINIUM   COLLECTION   10 July 1940

Any articles made of Aluminium or white metal may be taken to the Waiting Room on Friday next, July 12th, before 1 p.m.

G. B. Chetwynd-Stapylton,
Warden.

In order to economise in the use of paper, the printing of the annual village calendar was suspended for the duration of the war:

```
360 WEYBRIDGE.                                    23rd July 1940

                    N O T I C E.


        In view of the need for economy in paper the Trustees

     have decided not to issue a Whiteley Village Calendar for 1941.


                    G. B. Chetwynd-Stapylton,
                              Warden.
```

Villagers were often not as meticulous as they should have been in making sure that their cottages were properly blacked-out. Colonel Stapylton, the Warden, issued several notices reminding them of the importance of the black-out, culminating in the following:

```
     BLACK-OUT    PRECAUTIONS.
                                        23rd. August, 1940


        A little slit of light showing is sufficient to indicate
     to a hostile 'plane that it is over an inhabited area.
     Anyone showing a light therefore is guilty of an offence against
     his neighbours.   No excuse whatever  can be entertained for
     negligence in this respect and in future all offenders' lights
     will be removed for an indefinite period.

                    G. B. Chetwynd-Stapylton,

                              Warden.
```

The records unfortunately do not reveal whether the ultimate sanction of removing an offender's light-bulbs was ever actually resorted to!

In September 1940 the first (and only) official 'war injury' was sustained in the village. Sister Travis fell and broke her knee cap while hurrying to report an air-raid to Matron. The Trust's insurance company rejected her claim for accidental injury, describing it as a 'war injury' and recommending her to submit her claim to the Ministry of Pensions. The outcome of the matter is unfortunately not recorded; it is to be hoped she received the compensation to which she was entitled.

Not surprisingly, the Trustees found themselves unable to give their usual present of Christmas fare to villagers that year:

```
              N O T I C E.
                                        2nd, December 1940

        The Trustees regret that, owing to rationing restrictions,
     they are unable to distribute their customary gifts (in kind) this
     Christmas.

              They have decided, instead, to make each Villager a
     present of 5/- and this will be paid with the Allowances during
     the week ending 13th December 1940.

                    G. B. Chetwynd-Stapylton,
                              Warden
```

At that time, in late 1940, the London 'Blitz' was in full swing, and there can have been few nights when the air-raid warning was not sounded. The fire-watchers would have been on duty every night, and the air-raid shelters much used. They had by now been equipped with electric lights, which gave rise to the following notice:

```
                    N O T I C E.


    The electric light must not be left burning in the shelters

when they are unoccupied.

                            G. B. Chetwynd-Stapylton,

    29 Jan 1941                 Warden.
```

It seems a little surprising that, as the next notice indicates, it was not considered necessary to issue individual villagers with the means of fighting a fire until early in 1941:

```
                                      13th January 1941
        N O T I C E.

    For fighting incendiary bombs a half filled sandbag will

be delivered to every house shortly.

    Villagers are requested to turn the sand out in their porches

and to turn it over daily until quite dry, then to refill the

sandbag and keep it in the porch under cover.

                        G. B. Chetwynd-Stapylton,
```

Nevertheless, the village was not hit by any bombs during this period, and was to escape unscathed until much later in the war.

A poll held in 1941 for the village magazine asked the question, 'What subject concerns you most as a Villager?'. The reply was: Food – 99 per cent; Don't know – 1 per cent. Food was certainly very short at that time, but the residents of Whiteley Village were a good deal better off in this respect than many others. The communal kitchen, which had been set up in 1917 as a temporary measure to relieve the effect of shortages in the First World War, was still flourishing in September 1939, and under Bridget Nolan, the original cook, it continued to serve hot meals throughout the Second World War, Monday to Saturday, except Christmas Day and Boxing Day. Most villagers took their daily lunch from this kitchen, which meant that it was consistently providing about five thousand meals a month – an impressive achievement! Maintaining this service often meant, especially in the early months of the war, working through an air-raid, a risky practice made more dangerous by the fact that much of the roof was made of glass. Bridget, apparently, used to take refuge under a heavy marble-topped table when things got bad.

Unfortunately there are no records of what was served each day by this communal kitchen – no doubt Bridget did her best with the scanty rations available. What kept it going was the produce from the village farm. This 'farm' is unfortunately very poorly documented in the village records; what little is known about it is summarised in Appendix T. It is clear, however, that throughout the war it kept the communal kitchen almost completely supplied with vegetables, especially potatoes. This was undoubtedly an invaluable source of supply without which the kitchen might well have had to close. The meals must also have been very good value. At the start of the war, they cost 6d. each, but every villager received three free meal tickets a week. Amazingly, this price was held for the duration of the war.

The village magazine continued to be published throughout the war, but in reduced form in order to economise on paper which was in very short supply. It regularly contained tips on how to make clothes last longer (they were strictly rationed) and on how to make rations go further. There also used to be a morning B.B.C. programme called 'The Kitchen Front' on which economical recipes were given out by Freddie Grisewood, Mabel Constanduros and others. Some of these are given in Appendix U to illustrate what things were like at that time. The village magazine also helped to maintain morale by becoming noticeably lighter in tone than in previous years, with a definite sense of humour showing through in the 'home-produced' section, small though it was.

The village cinema in the hall continued throughout the war showing a mixture of feature films, Ministry of Information programmes and Pathe newsreels. Occasionally the hall was let by the Trustees for concerts for the troops, villagers being allowed to take up any spare seats:

```
WEYBRIDGE.
                        N O T I C E.                    22nd. November, 19

          The Village Hall has been lent by the Trustees to the
     Troops for a Concert at 2.30 p.m. on Sunday, 23rd. November.
          Through the kindness of the Commanding Officer a limited
     number of seats are being reserved for Villagers who can only
     be admitted by ticket.         Tickets may be applied for at the
     Stores but only a few are available.
                             G. B. Chetwynd-Stapylton,
                                     Warden.
```

Early in 1942, due to a cut in the petrol ration, the bus service had to be restricted even further:

```
                   B U S      S E R V I C E

         In future, to save petrol, the Dennis Coach will not call
     at the Railway Station on the return journey from Walton unless
     previously requested.
                             G. B. Chetwynd-Stapylton,
                                     Warden.
```

```
                                               2nd June, 1942.

            VILLAGE   OMNIBUS.


     Owing to the curtailment of the service no name may be
put down for the bus more often than once a fortnight.

                              G. B. Chatwynd-Stapylton,
                                    Warden.
```

The Trustees also reduced their regular meetings from twelve to six times a year in order to economise on travel in response to the slogan 'Is your journey really necessary?'

A little later that year a special salvage drive was held:

```
360 WEYBRIDGE.                              14th July, 1942.

            S A L V A G E.
       VERY   URGENT

A special Salvage drive is being held in this District next week.
The situation as regards shipping and the supply of Raw Materials
is VERY SERIOUS INDEED.
        Please put out every bit you can spare of Rubber, Rags
and Metals for the Dustman.
        All paper that can possibly be spared (e.g. newspapers,
brown paper, magazines, books etc.) should be brought to the
Waiting Room on Monday 20th instant.

                              G. B. Chetwynd-Stapylton,
                                    Warden.
```

Although by this time the Blitz had finished, air-raids remained a common occurrence, and villagers still had to be reminded of the need to be vigilant about their black-out precautions:

```
                   N O T I C E.
     There is much laxity in blacking-out throughout the Village.
     The greatest care must still be exercised.   Torches must
     be pointed direct on to the ground.  G. B. Chetwynd-Stapylton,
                                                Warden.
```

The fire-watchers kept vigil every night, as the extract from the October 1942 edition of the village magazine (Appendix V) shows.

With a good number of staff away on active service or doing war work, the village was very short-staffed. Matron found that, although she had a full complement of sisters, she only had half the established number of nurses, maids and charwomen; with the result that the hospital staff found they could not cope properly. The office staff helped out, but it still proved very difficult to keep the place running. It was generally very difficult throughout the war to obtain staff for work not directly related to the war effort, with many more jobs available than people willing to fill them. In an endeavour to rectify the situation, the Trustees made a substantial increase in staff wages in 1941, but this proved only partly successful, and the village remained short of staff throughout this period.

As the war progressed, the need for economy intensified. So did the need for assistance for refugees, and frequent appeals were made:

BRING and BUY for The RED CROSS   Oct. 1944

A "BRING and BUY" effort is being held in the Village – to make a gift in cash to the British Red Cross Society before Christmas.

Everyone in the Village, man, woman and child, is being asked to help by bringing a home-made article to either Matron or Miss Taylor during the first week in November. These will then be priced, and a sale will be held the following week at which everyone will be asked to buy one article.

Gifts should therefore be simple and inexpensive, and should in no case cost more than 5/-. Rationed goods (things bought in shops on coupons, etc.) are not allowed. Any handicraft, garden produce, etc., would be suitable.

All proceeds will be handed over to the British Red Cross Society on behalf of the Village.

Although the village (only some thirty miles from London) escaped the Blitz in late 1940 and early 1941, the estate was hit twice within eight days by bombs in mid-1944. On 21 August two bombs fell on the land to the south of Fox Oak adjoining Seven Hills Road. The only damage caused was to some of the windows in the southern end of Fox Oak. Then, just over a week later, on 29 August, another bomb landed in the hollow ground behind the village shelter on Strawberry Hill. This bomb did much more damage, although again, luckily, no-one was hurt. A total of 97 buildings in the village suffered some damage, from wrenched door-latches to broken windows and fallen ceilings.

On 4 May 1945 the Germans surrendered to Field Marshal Montgomery on Luneburg Heath, and three days later signed a general capitulation at Rheims. On the same day the WV Fire Guard Service was disbanded:

```
                                                7th May, 1945.


           F I R E   G U A R D S.


   The Fire Guard Service has now been disbanded.   Fire Guards,
who desire to do so, may retain their steel helmets, arm bands
and eye shields.
        Any of this equipment which it is not desired to retain
may please be returned to the office by Thursday next 10th inst.

                        G. B. Chetwynd-Stapylton,
                            Warden.
```

It was, however, not until considerably later that villagers were told to remove their black-out:

```
                                          20th June, 1945.
               N O T I C E S.


BLACK-OUT
            Villagers are requested to remove their black-out
        both in the interest of health and cleanliness and
        to economise in light.


CINEMA      The Cinema will be discontinued during the months
        of July, August and September.


POLLING
DAY.        Arrangements are being made to take voters to
        the poll in the Village bus.



CHIMNEY
SWEEPING.   Chimney sweeping will begin on Monday, June 25th
        in Section A, No. 1 and will continue in rotation.
        Those who decline the services of the sweep, or are
        absent for the day, must make their own arrangements
        for chimney sweeping until the end of the present year.
                        G. B. Chetwynd-Stapylton,
                            Warden.
```

47. Col G. P. Chetwynd – Stapleton, CBE, OBE, TD, DL (the second Warden).

Staff who had been away on active service or doing war work returned to the village during the second half of 1945, thus easing the staffing situation.

In the January 1946 New Year's Honours List, the Warden, Colonel Chetwynd-Stapylton, was awarded the OBE in recognition of his services to the welfare of troops stationed locally throughout the war. In the February 1946 edition of the village magazine, the chaplain wrote:

To-day's issue of 'The Times' announces that our Warden, Colonel Chetwynd-Stapylton, has been honoured by the King with the OBE. We rejoice in his well-earned distinction because we of all people know how richly he deserves it. His service of the welfare of the troops took heavy toll of his time and strength, yet he did not fail in constant thought for the village.

In January 1946, the Chairman of the Trustees, the Rt Hon and Rt Revd Arthur Foley Winnington-Ingram, PC, KCVO, DD, Lord Bishop of London, celebrated his 88th birthday. A telegram of congratulations was sent:

```
    360 WEYBRIDGE.                                          26th January

                            N O T I C E.


        The following telegram has to-day been sent to our

    Chairman on the occasion of his 88th birthday:-

            BISHOP  WINNINGTON  INGRAM,

                  CRAG  HEAD  HOTEL,

                      BOURNEMOUTH.


        Many happy returns.
```

His health had, however, been failing for some time, and a little later that year, on 26 May, he died. The following obituary written by Lord Daryngton, one of his fellow Trustees, appeared in the June 1946 edition of the village magazine:

> The late Lord Bishop of London, Dr Winnington-Ingram, Chairman of the Trustees of Whiteley Village, has passed over and we who are left behind deplore his loss but trust that we may worthily continue the policy which he so surely enshrined.
>
> As one who has had the great privilege of close association with him and always viewed with affectionate regard the work that he accomplished as a teacher and a friend, I wish to give my humble testimony as to the value of his influence not only in the Church of England but on Christendom.
>
> He was everyone's friend, from the members of the Royal Circle to the humblest little boy or girl in a home of Waifs and Strays Society, of which he was the illustrious Chairman.
>
> As a speaker he was eminent, not only as a preacher but as one who replied to interrupters in mass meetings on Tower Hill.
>
> Those who knew him in Whiteley Village realised his humanity, his sense of humour, broadmindedness, affability and self-sacrificing service, and we realised the help he gave in making the village what it is.
>
> He won a First Class at his University, but to his mind it did not matter much whether a man or woman was clever or not so long as there was sufficient cleverness to know what really matters in the world.
>
> God grant that we may follow his example and keep as a precious memory the fact of his energy, faith, perseverance and lovableness.

The first Trustees' garden party for seven years was planned for 22 June 1946, and the band of the East Surrey Regiment booked to play. However, rationing restrictions were still very severe, and no caterer could be found able and willing to tender for providing the tea. Even Harrods declined. The Trustees therefore felt obliged to postpone the resumption of their annual garden party for yet another year, until 1947. This decision may have been influenced by the deaths of Bishop Winnington-Ingram, and also of another long-serving and greatly respected Trustee, Sir Arthur Sackville Trevor Griffith-Boscawen, PC, MP, on 1 June 1946.

Several other people who had links with Whiteley Village also died during this period, notably:

Major the Hon Francis Stewart-Mackenzie, a Trustee and nephew of Col Brodrick, who was killed on active service in North Africa in 1943.

Mr Arthur D. Ingram, the first Secretary to the Trustees from 1907 to 1935, who died in January 1945.

Sir George Barnes, a Trustee, who died in late 1946.

Sir John Oakley, the original surveyor to the Trustees, who also died in late 1946.

Although the war was over, the country still faced a period of great austerity and, if anything, food rationing became even more severe than it had been during the war. Bread rationing was introduced for the first time. The village shop was unable to cope with the extra work-load:

```
                                              11th July, 1946.

            B R E A D   R A T I O N I N G.

    ALL  THOSE  WHO  HAVE  BEEN  BUYING  THEIR  BREAD  AT  THE
VILLAGE  STORES  ARE  ASKED  TO  MAKE  ARRANGEMENTS  TO  OBTAIN
IT  AFTER  21st  JULY  FROM  ONE  OR  OTHER  OF  THE  BAKERS
WHO  DELIVER  IN  THE  VILLAGE.
    IT  IS  WITH  THE  GREATEST  REGRET  THAT  IT  HAS  BEEN
FOUND  NECESSARY  TO  MAKE  THIS  REQUEST  BUT  IT  IS  IMPOSSIBLE
TO  DEAL  WITH  THE  EXTRA  WORK  ENVOLVED  IN  ACCOUNTING  FOR
BREAD  COUPONS.
                    FLOUR  AND  CAKES  HOWEVER  WILL  STILL  BE
SOLD  AT  THE  STORES.
                              G. B. Chetwynd-Stapylton.
```

On 30 June 1946, a double tragedy struck the village. Alec Moody (one of the estate workers and son of the estate foreman) and Gordon Maynard (son of the village plumber) drowned in the River Mole. The exact circumstances of what happened are not entirely clear, but the two of them appear to have been taking part in a Sunday afternoon outing from the village to the river, during which young Maynard went for a swim and got into difficulties. Alec Moody then followed him in to try and save him, but failed and lost his own life as well.

On 28 June 1947, the first post-war Trustees' garden party was held. During the day, three memorial tablets were unveiled in St Mark's church. Two of these were placed on the north wall: the first was in memory of George King and John Wallace, who had died whilst prisoners-of-war in 1943; the second was in memory of Alec Moody and Gordon Maynard; the third tablet was placed in the chancel and commemorates Bishop Winnington-Ingram. A silver memorial chalice and paten were also presented to St Mark's in memory of the late Bishop who had done so much for the Trust. The money for these had been raised by the villagers through donations not only of cash but of small articles of silver to be melted down and incorporated into the chalice.

There is a fourth tablet in St Mark's, on the north wall. This is dedicated to W/Off. Messenger, and was unveiled on 10 March 1949 by Bishop Golding-Bird. (The text of all four tablets is given in Appendix W.)

Despite its proximity to London, Whiteley Village and its residents had survived the war virtually unscathed and now, in common with the rest of the country, looked forward to a period of prolonged peace and of increasing prosperity.

Chapter Nine

THE POST-WAR YEARS (1948-64)

'Fings ain't what they used to be' could well serve as the subtitle for this chapter. It was a period of change, and of adjustment to declining standards. The main cause was financial. On the one hand the cost of maintaining the village and its many facilities to the original high standards and to which the residents had become accustomed rose inexorably; on the other hand the income to the Trust from its investment portfolio (which was then its only source of income) actually declined. This was not really a new situation. As early as 1936 the Trustees had had to choose between erecting more cottages at the end of Hornbeam Walk and building a new office in the village because they could not afford both, and had chosen the latter because of the savings that they would be able to make by closing the London office when the new village office opened. At that time the need to make such a choice did not seem a very serious matter, and when war broke out a few years later the financial problem was pushed into the background while wartime concerns took precedence. After the war, however, the situation could no longer be ignored, and something had to be done.

The running costs for the village had always been substantial, with staff wages accounting for the major part of the annual expenditure. During the war labour had been scarce, and higher pay had been one way of attracting the staff needed to run the village. Other employers had also raised their wages in order to get the staff they needed, and the Trust was increasingly forced to take account of local and national rates in setting its own wage levels. The new National Insurance Act, introduced as part of the legislation which created the welfare state, added to the Trust's employment costs.

Increasing employment costs were only part of the problem. The bus service, laundry, stores, and communal kitchen were also costing more to run, as were the hospital and home of rest. The cottages and other buildings in the village were also needing more spent on them to keep them in good order.

At the same time, the income from the Trust's investment portfolio was actually declining. The main reason for this lay in a combination of circumstances. In his will Mr Whiteley had laid down (in Clause 39 – see Appendix A) quite restrictive terms governing the way in which the Trust's money could be invested. At the time he wrote his will the railways, docks and harbours, gas, water and other similar companies which he specified must have seemed absolutely secure. He could not have foreseen the nationalisation programme of the post-war Labour government and the effect that that would have on share values in such companies or on the income derived from them. It is to the credit of the Trustees that, in the early stages of the government's programme, they managed to avoid the serious losses many investors suffered from the nationalisation of the railways and the electrical industry by selling their shares in those enterprises at an early stage and re-investing the money in other stocks permitted by the will whose value had not yet been affected by nationalisation. It had, however, become clear to the Trustees that urgent action was needed to give them wider discretion as to the investments which the Trust might hold, and an approach was made to the Charity Commissioners seeking permission for this. Eventually this was granted – many other Charities had made a similar approach – but the legal process was a slow one, and it was not finally approved until the summer of 1952. Meanwhile, the Trust's income had continued to decline and its expenditure to rise. It then took some years for advantage to be taken of the new arrangement, and for the resulting improvement to be felt, after which the situation improved for a number of years. Appendix X summarises the excesses of expenditure over income and vice-versa for this period.

The villagers themselves began to benefit from the new welfare state that was being created by the post-war Labour government, especially with regard to the new state old-age pensions that were introduced. This had been fixed at 26s. (£1.30) per week each. Then, in 1950, it was increased for those with no other income by another 5s. (25p) a week for a single person and by 7s. 6d. (37½p) a week for a married couple. In view of this, and after much discussion, the Trustees decided to introduce a maintenance charge of 2s. 6d. (12½p) a week for single villagers and 3s. 9d. (about 18p) a week for married couples from 3 July 1950. In doing so, the Trustees took great care, with the co-operation of the National Assistance Board, that no villager suffered hardship as a result of having to pay these charges. From 1 February 1954, the charges were renamed 'amenity charges' and were increased to 10s. (50p) per week for single villagers, and 15s. (75p) per week for married couples. However, these new 'amenity charges' only applied to those entering the village on or after 1 February 1954; all those who had been resident before that date continued to pay the 'maintenance charge' at the old rate. This unequal arrangement lasted until 1 April 1956 when all villagers were required to pay the new 'amenity charges', which were then regularly reviewed. Appendix Y shows how the charges were increased over the years.

This new source of income was a great help in easing the Trust's financial difficulties, but economies were also needed, and some of the pre-war traditions, which had been suspended for the duration, were either never reinstated or were restarted on a more economical basis. For example, the publication of a village calendar was not restarted, and the annual Trustees' garden party, although it continued, became a much less formal event, partly due to the need for economy and partly due to changing times. A military band was still a regular fixture at this event but, as one villager commented somewhat mournfully in the village magazine (March 1961), the days of '... the marquee on the green and Harrods' gilt chairs and all that ...' were gone. Other economies followed. The communal kitchen had been losing money for some years (Bridget Nolan had retired in 1951 and had been succeeded by a Mrs Taylor) and in 1954 it was decided to close the kitchen on two days of the week – Mondays and Saturdays – in an effort to reduce losses.

Village life had nevertheless been going on much as usual. People dropped litter, and the Warden asked them not to:

17th March 1948

NOTICE

THE VILLAGE IS LOOKING VERY UNTIDY BY REASON OF THE LITTER (WASTE PAPER, CIGARETTE CARTONS ETC.) THAT IS BEING THROWN ABOUT EVERYWHERE. PLEASE ABSTAIN FROM THIS THOUGHTLESS AND DEGRADING PRACTICE AND PREVENT OTHERS FROM MARRING THE BEAUTY OF OUR VILLAGE IN THIS WAY.

G. B. Chetwynd-Stapylton
Warden

He also asked them to economise in the use of electricity (which the Trust was then paying for!):

30th September 1948

NOTICE

DURING THE WINTER MONTHS, IT IS OF VITAL NATIONAL IMPORTANCE THAT EVERY ECONOMY IN THE USE OF ELECTRIC LIGHT SHALL BE EXERCISED. EVERYBODY IS THEREFORE ASKED TO DO THEIR UTMOST TO KEEP THE CONSUMPTION OF ELECTRICITY DOWN. PLEASE SEE THAT ALL LIGHTS NOT IMMEDIATELY REQUIRED ARE TURNED OUT.

G. B. Chetwynd-Stapylton
Warden

The rationing of food and other commodities went on for some time after the end of the war, with all the extra administration that that entailed, as the next notice shows:

23rd November 1948

NOTICE

WHEN PATIENTS ARE ADMITTED TO HOSPITAL IT IS NECESSARY FOR THEM TO BRING THEIR RATION BOOKS. CLOTHING BOOKS, PERSONAL POINTS, PENSION BOOKS AND IDENTITY CARDS WITH THEM.

THESE ARE KEPT IN SAFE CUSTODY BY THE MATRON ON THEIR BEHALF AND RETURNED TO THE PATIENTS ON DISCHARGE.

G. B. Chetwynd-Stapylton
Warden

Constant reviews of prices, as well as of the newly introduced village 'amenity charge' were essential to cope with inflation, and the communal kitchen was no exception:

3rd June 1952

NOTICE

THE TRUSTEES HAVE DECIDED THAT IT HAS BECOME NECESSARY TO RAISE
THE PRICE OF DINNERS FROM 8d. TO 1/-. FROM THE 30th JUNE 1952
THEREFORE, THE COST OF THE MEAT AND VEGETABLE COURSE WILL BE 8d. AND OF THE SWEET COURSE 4d.

G. B. Chetwynd-Stapylton
Warden

Television really arrived in Whiteley Village in 1953, just in time for the coronation of Queen Elizabeth II. Two T.V. sets were ordered; a large one for the hall and a smaller one for the hospital. The coronation was a major event for the village that year – the televising of the actual ceremony formed only part of almost a week of festivities. Coronation day itself fell on Tuesday 2 June and was no doubt viewed on television by most of the village. On Thursday the Trustees provided a band to play on the Green:

27th May 1953

CORONATION

ON THURSDAY, 4th JUNE 1953 THE BUGLE BAND OF THE 4th/5th CADET BATTALION THE EAST SURREY REGIMENT WILL BEAT RETREAT ON THE GREEN AT 7.30 P.M. AND WILL MARCH PAST IN FRONT OF THE TERRACE STEPS ON CONCLUSION OF THE PARADE.

G. B. Chetwynd-Stapylton
Warden

Then on Friday evening at the hall there was a 'Coronation Dance'; while on the following Tuesday and Wednesday (9 and 10 June) there were coach trips from the village to view the coronation illuminations in London.

By the mid-1950s, Whiteley Village had been 'open' for almost forty years but no villagers had yet lived to be 100. This changed on 17 May 1956 when Mrs Elizabeth Matthews became Whiteley Village's first centenarian. Mrs Matthews had come to Whiteley Village from Yorkshire with her husband in October 1925 when they moved into 11 South Avenue. Tragically, her husband died only a month later. Mrs Matthews then moved to 3 Circle Road, where she lived until 1952, when at the age of 96 she exchanged her 'upstairs cottage' for a room in Whiteley House (then, still the home of rest). Her centenary was marked by telegrams from the Queen and the Trustees. She received many gifts of fruit, flowers, cards and other presents and was given a special birthday tea in the village hall at which a birthday cake complete with a hundred candles was presented to her. Mrs Matthews easily succeeded in blowing them all out. She went on to celebrate several more birthdays in similar style until she died on 5 September 1961 at the age of 105, having become the oldest villager to date and having lived in the village for almost 36 years.

1956 also saw the end of the Executive Committee of Trustees that had been in existence for some 38 years (1918-56). Since 28 June 1947, the meetings of the Executive Committee had been open to all Trustees, regardless of whether the Trustee had been especially appointed to this body. Thus, since that date there was no real difference between the Executive Committee and the general body of Trustees. In June 1956 Sir John Wenham proposed and the Trustees resolved to rescind the resolution of 16 October 1918 which had established the Executive Committee.

The lack of money remained a cause of major concern to the Trustees throughout the late 1950s and into the 1960s. Fox Oak, the Warden's residence, was becoming increasingly expensive to maintain and the idea of selling this property was discussed as early as 1957. The idea had been rejected as it was estimated that the money

48. Mrs Matthews on her 105th birthday.

raised from its sale balanced against the cost of building a new Warden's residence would all but cancel each other out. A new proposal was put forward later that year, however, to convert part of Fox Oak into a flat to be leased privately. This was done at a cost of about £1,500 and was leased to a Miss U. Jackson at the end of 1958. The flat thus brought in a small income for the Trust for a few years, but a change of Warden and improvements in the property market raised the matter of Fox Oak's sale again only a few years later. Colonel Stapylton retired in July 1959 and was succeeded by Mr P. G. Hunt who had come to Whiteley Village as Trust Secretary only two years earlier. On his appointment as Warden, the post of Trust Secretary ceased to exist. By 1961 it had been decided that Fox Oak was no longer a suitable residence for the Warden, '... it was not from any point of view a practical house to run ...'. It was then agreed that Fox Oak Cottage, previously the stable block to Fox Oak, should be converted to become the Warden's house. Some consideration was given to converting Fox Oak into several flats for letting, but this idea did not get much support from the Trustees. Their opinions were possibly coloured by the fact that Miss Jackson, the occupant of the Fox Oak flat, was at the time several months in arrears with her rent. Early in 1963 it was decided to sell Fox Oak, and this was done by auction on 10 July 1963. It realised the sum of £18,500 (only about two and

49. Mr P. G. Hunt (the third Warden).

a half times what the Trust had paid for the house in 1912).

With the new Warden came other changes in the village. The 'Rules and Regulations' became 'Terms of Residence', and in 1960 the home of rest was re-named Whiteley House. The 1960s also saw other changes to 'village institutions'. In May 1963, fares were re-introduced on the village bus – the rate was 3d. per journey (6d. return). It is not known how the village managed to overcome the problem of requiring a special licence if fares were charged. By 1963, the fact that Mr Cooke and Mr Coote had both been fined 2s. 6d. for such an offence in 1934 had obviously been forgotten. A year later in May 1964 the village laundry was closed and the laundry services were contracted out while the Trustees considered the installation of a village launderette.

That same year it was reluctantly decided to close the communal kitchen. Maintaining this service had become increasingly costly to the Trust over the years. The kitchen served its last meal on Friday, 28 October 1966.

The end of 1963 saw the dedication of the village's third church. The Roman Catholics of the village, always relatively few in number, had for many years been taken to a local RC church on Sundays and holy days (initially this had been in Weybridge, but later became Hersham). The idea of using St Mark's 'Chapel of Rest' as a Roman Catholic chapel seems to have come from the village chaplain, the Revd Sinker. In June 1963, he told the Trustees how delighted he was with the co-operation that existed between himself, the sanctuary minister and Roman Catholic priest, and that he had discussed with the latter the possibility of the St Mark's Chapel of Rest being used as a Roman Catholic chapel. He went on to tell them that Father Hayes was approaching his bishop and it was hoped he would agree. The Trustees were in full agreement with this suggestion and Father Hayes' bishop evidently approved too, because the Catholic chapel of the Most Holy Family was dedicated in a special service on 22 December 1963.

1961 also saw some changes to the landscaping of the village. The trees that ran in front of the houses in West Avenue (and East Avenue) were removed to allow more light into the cottages. Some of the shrubbery was also removed from around the village, provoking the following comment in the March 1961 edition of the village magazine: 'It is nice to see East Avenue at long last. All the undergrowth surrounding it has kept it so much in the background that we rather had the impression at times it did not exist'.

The village cinema continued through the '50s and '60s, although from October 1961 the weekly film shows were reduced to fortnightly shows owing to smaller audiences, apparently because the films were not as good as they used to be.

A Whiteley Village 'League of Friends' was formed in June 1963 with the purpose of raising funds for village amenities. Sadly, it was short-lived and closed in December 1966.

The Whiteley Village Association was established in August 1960 '... to maintain and further financially or otherwise the social activities and interests of residents in Whiteley Village ...'. All residents of Whiteley Village were automatically made members, and no membership fee was charged, although by July 1963 it was felt necessary to ask members to contribute 1d. per week to help maintain the Association's funds, it being stressed that this was *not* a subscription and that members could not be forced to pay this sum.

The Association had an Executive Committee which comprised: the Warden as president, the Warden's assistant as vice-president, an honorary secretary, an honorary treasurer, 12 members representing the various clubs that existed in the village, and two additional 'independent' members. The Association continues to this day.

On several occasions throughout this period, the Trustees reluctantly considered plans to sell or re-develop some of the outlying land owned by the Trust, particularly the areas adjoining Seven Hills Road and Burwood Road, because of the ever-present need to find extra income. In 1955 there had been approaches to the Trust by an oil company to lease or buy an area of land adjoining Seven Hills Road with the purpose of erecting a petrol filling station, but Walton Council refused planning permission. In 1963 the principal of the National College of Food Technology approached Mr Hunt to enquire whether the Trustees would be willing to lease High Park as a playing field for the college. A lease was drawn up and the college used High Park until 1965 when the University of Reading took over the lease. The leasing of High Park as a playing field obviously gave the Trustees ideas for obtaining extra income without having to sell or develop the land. The recreation ground was leased to the Hawks Hockey Club in 1966. The village farm was then gradually run down and the land released made available for other sports clubs that were looking for playing fields; the Old Reedonians, Old Ardinians, Old Bradfieldians and Old Salopians were all granted leases.

Towards the end of this period, it became increasingly clear that the standard of accommodation offered in the village fell far short of modern expectation. The Warden, Peter Hunt, was keenly aware of this, and did his utmost, within the limitations of a strict budget, to make the cottages more attractive and to improve the other premises. Largely as a result of his efforts, the Trustees began to make plans to modernise the whole village, and a Modernisation Sub-Committee was formed in mid-1962 to consider this issue and other related matters. The result was a comprehensive modernisation programme lasting several years.

Chapter Ten

MODERNISATION (1962-70)

By the early 1960s most of the buildings in the village were nearly 50 years old, and were beginning to show their age. A shortage of maintenance staff, particularly painters, both during and after the war meant that there had been an almost continuous backlog of work throughout that period, and many cottages were looking somewhat neglected. Many of the fixtures and fittings inside the cottages and around the village were out-of-date and in need of replacement. The open coal fires in the cottages were also out-of-date. They were labour-intensive to run, in terms of both the staff required to deliver the coal and the villagers themselves who had to get their coal in, keep their fire stoked, and clear away the ash afterwards. They were also dirty, creating a great deal of ash, dust, smoke, and smuts. Another consideration was that by then open coal fires had become a very expensive method of heating.

The Trustees had recognised the need for a substantial modernisation programme when they formed their Modernisation Sub-Committee in mid-1962. Their main problem was how to finance such a large undertaking. The Warden, Peter Hunt, had suggested as early as 1961 that a public appeal might be made, but the Trustees had rejected his proposal on the grounds that it was not really a practical proposition. However, the sale of Fox Oak in 1963 raised a useful sum which gave impetus to their plans and enabled a start to be made.

The first requirement, which also had a bearing on the type of heating to be installed in the cottages to replace the open coal fires, was to relay all the electrical cables in the village. The rise in the level of domestic electricity consumption after the war had not been foreseen, and the original cables were simply not big enough to carry all the current that was now being consumed in the village. As early as 1954 the Warden had had to appeal to villagers to economise in the use of electricity:

5th May 1954

ELECTRICITY SUPPLY

FOR REASONS OF ECONOMY, AND ALSO BECAUSE THE WIRING SYSTEM THROUGHOUT THE VILLAGE CANNOT STAND UP TO ANY ABNORMAL INCREASE OF LOAD, PERMISSION FOR THE USE OF VARIOUS ELECTRIC GADGETS IN THE COTTAGES CANNOT BE GRANTED. RESTRICTED USE OF ELECTRIC IRONS AND SMALL VACUUM CLEANERS MAY BE ALLOWED IN THE MORNINGS BUT NOT DURING THE EVENING PEAK LOAD PERIOD. IN ANY CASE, ANY APPARATUS WHICH IT IS PROPOSED TO USE MUST BE PASSED BY THE ELECTRICIAN

G. B. Chetwynd-Stapylton
Warden

119

and had to continue to remind them of the need for economy from time-to-time:

19th January 1955

ELECTRICITY SUPPLY

ATTENTION IS DRAWN TO THE NOTICE OF 5th MAY 1954 RESTRICTING THE USE OF GADGETS.

VILLAGERS ARE EARNESTLY REQUESTED TO OBSERVE THESE RESTRIC-TIONS LOYALLY AND SO AVOID THE POSSIBILITY OF A BREAK-DOWN IN THE VILLAGE SUPPLY. IT IS REGRETTED THAT THE USE OF ELECTRIC FIRES CANNOT BE AUTHORISED.

G. B. Chetwynd-Stapylton
Warden

Approaches were therefore made to the South Eastern Electricity Board regarding the contribution the Trust would be expected to make towards the renewal of the electric cabling round the village. The Board initially asked for £9,000 to £10,000, but the Trustees were adamant that they were not prepared to pay more than £6,000, and eventually agreement was reached on a price of £4,244 plus a reconnection charge of £7 per building. Work began in March 1964. In May the village magazine commented that the village was beginning to resemble '... the fields of Flanders in 1914-1918'. That was but a foretaste of what was to come; builders and workmen were to be an integral part of village life for the next six years.

Now that work had actually started the Trustees, through their Modernisation Sub-Committee, began to make proper plans for the work that needed to be done, and to raise the money needed to finance it. It quickly became apparent that the amount of work required would be such that it would not be practical, or economical, to work upon cottages on an individual basis, and that it would be necessary to work on two or three rows of cottages at a time. This raised the problem of how to accommodate a considerable number of villagers while their cottages were being refurbished. Mr Hunt suggested that an annex to Whiteley House should be built for this purpose, with the dual purpose of providing the temporary accommodation needed to house villagers while their cottages were being worked on, and then sub-sequently to be used to provide permanent accommodation for additional residents so as to increase the Trust's income. At first, the Trustees viewed this proposal with some scepticism, but when they had given the matter further consideration, they decided to adopt it. In May 1965 a firm of architects called Ley Colbeck and Partners was selected to draw up plans for this 'dormitory' building, together with a standard plan for the modernisation of the cottages. Mr Tony Abel, one of the partners, was appointed by his firm to deal with village affairs, thus beginning a relationship which was to last for more than 25 years.

Ley Colbeck and Partners worked fast and the plans for the dormitory building were presented to the Trustees in July 1965 and accepted. It was anticipated that the building would cost about £73,000 – partly depending on the type of heating to be installed. There was then a short delay while the necessary finance was raised and while the plans were put out to tender. In April 1966 the Trustees felt able to proceed and accepted the lowest tender of £66,795 from Gaze's of Walton for its construction. This was considered a very good price by the Trustees; no doubt they benefited from the fact that Government restrictions on building work at that time had made the trade fiercely competitive. To help finance the project, the Trust received a grant from the Ministry of Housing of £15 a year for each room, which was to continue until the building became registered for occupation by permanent residents.

The Trustees had by now also accepted Ley Colbeck's plans for modernising the cottages, but had decided to begin by refurbishing one cottage only on a trial basis to see how the plans worked in practice. Cottage No. A5 was selected for the trial, and in July 1966 the Trustees accepted Gaze's tender of £1,805 for the work to be done. The local council gave a 'Home Improvement Grant' of £258 towards this cost.

By January 1967 the dormitory building had been completed, and the Trustees decided to call it Ingram House in memory of the first Chairman of the Trustees. A5 had been completed too, and had been approved by the Trustees, so everything was ready for the main modernisation programme to start. It was estimated that this would take between five and six years to complete, and that it would cost about £500,000 – just about what it had cost to build the village in the first place!

Towards the end of June 1967 the residents of section A moved to Ingram House so that work on their cottages could begin. A removal van was purchased by the Trust to help move all their furniture. Some villagers chose to go and stay with relatives or friends for a while, and the usual rules about how long they could be away from the village were relaxed for that year.

By December 1967 work on A section was almost complete, and the residents began moving back into their refurbished cottages. It was at this point that some hitherto unforeseen problems arose concerning the alterations that had been made, despite the trial that had been carried out on A5. The plan for the cottages in the section had involved doing away with the bed-recess altogether. The old kitchen had been extended to become a bedroom, which led on to a larger modern toilet and shower area, while the old bed-recess had been turned into a new kitchen. The trouble was that the size of the furniture owned by some of the residents had not been taken into account. The new layout provided less space for large items of furniture, and quite a few of the residents had bulky Victorian cabinets and wardrobes which they treasured. It was also found that the closing-off of the bed recess cut out some of the light entering the cottages. Previously, there had been a window at each end of the combined living-room/bed recess which had meant that some sunlight entered the cottage during the day, whatever its aspect. This was no longer the case. As a result, Ley Colbeck prepared a 'second revised' plan which included a bed recess and therefore effectively went back to the original design. This was adopted, and proved to be about £55 cheaper than the first plan! (See Appendix Z for the details of these plans.)

These were not the only problems that had to be overcome. In an article published in the *Architect and Building News* on 10 April 1969, Mr Abel said that the great problem architecturally was that though in principle the cottages are the same throughout

... they vary in detail to a terrific extent. For example, some cottages have side-hung casement windows, some have sliding sashes, and some even have horizontal sliding windows. Again, the provision of built-in cupboards varies throughout the village, as does the size of chimney breasts and the recesses at the sides of these. We aimed to standardise the modernisation as much as possible but such were the variations we found that every cottage practically has had to be dealt with separately.

Something of an exaggeration, perhaps, but maybe not too surprising when it is remembered that the cottages had been designed by no less than seven different architects.

Work now continued apace. By October 1969 A, B and J sections had been completed, and, as a result of the revision of the plan made after the work on A Section had been completed, the work had cost almost £8,500 less than had originally been estimated. By January 1970 C section had been completed, and work rapidly proceeded in D, G, E and H sections. F section came last. By July that had also been completed, and every cottage had been modernised and re-occupied.

The inevitable loss of some of the original features of the cottages was not always popular. The replacement of conventional doors by sliding doors inside the cottages as a space-saving measure attracted very little adverse comment, but some villagers found it inconvenient having no back door, while others regretted the loss of a bath and its replacement by a shower. Others missed their open fires. However, although some villagers were critical, especially at the beginning, and lamented the passing of the old-style cottages, most of them were pleased with what had been done and quickly forgot the inconvenience of the move to Ingram House and back. As one of those who lived in a cottage which was renovated fairly early in the programme commented soon after returning, '... they haven't forgotten a thing in the new Cottages. When I go to visit a friend in one of the old ones I really notice the difference ...'.

A statement setting out the costs of the cottage modernisation programme is in Appendix AA. From the notes to that Appendix (which is an extract from a report presented to the Trustees early in 1971) it will be seen that the programme included the conversion of the staff house in G section to form three new cottages (G27, G28 and G29), alterations to F section staff house and alterations to the staff flats in 39 and 39a Circle Road. Although the cost was not included in that report to the Trustees, the club, hall, and stores had also been given a 'face-lift' while the work on the cottages was going on.

In the light of the financial problems which they had faced during the previous 15 years it was a bold decision on the part of the Trustees to proceed with the modernisation programme when they did. It was undoubtedly the right decision, however, because it firmly re-established the village as a viable concern for many years to come. Sadly, one notable village 'landmark' was lost during this period. Sometime in the summer of 1967, the *green* pillar-box outside the village stores (which may well have been the only green pillar-box left in the country) was painted red by the post office, to the disappointment of many.

EPILOGUE

With the completion of the modernisation programme in 1971, Whiteley Village entered upon what can well be regarded as the 'second stage' of its life which, it was hoped, would last well into the next century. Although there would undoubtedly be many more changes and improvements needed in the future to keep it in good order and to meet the ever-increasing expectations of its residents, it was then, and still remains to this day, a role model in its provision for the elderly, particularly as regards its ability to care for its residents to the end of their lives.

This 'second stage' of the village's life lies beyond the scope of this book. Suffice to say that the late 1980s and early 1990s were to see some significant challenges and changes which, it is to be hoped, someone else will chronicle in the future. For my part, it has been a wonderful experience to have lived and worked in the village these past few years.

Alan Brown
Warden (in succession to Peter Hunt)
Fox Oak Cottage
Whiteley Village
February 1992

THE WHITELEY HOMES.

EXTRACTS from the WILL of
WILLIAM WHITELEY, Esqre., deceased.

Proved 16th April, 1907.

16.—I DIRECT that my General Trustees or Trustee shall out of the money to arise from the sale and conversion of my said residuary real and personal estate and out of my ready money in the first place pay my funeral and testamentary expenses and debts and pay or provide for the legacies (including the two legacies or sums of £50,000 hereinbefore bequeathed in trust as aforesaid) and annuities hereby or by any Codicil hereto bequeathed and also all estate legacy and other duties payable in respect of my estate and the said legacies and annuities or otherwise payable under this my Will And shall in the next place set apart and appropriate out of the said residuary monies two several sums or trust legacies of £5,000 and £5,000 to be held upon the trusts and subject to the powers and provisions hereinafter declared and contained concerning the same respectively and subject as aforesaid I declare that my General Trustees or Trustee shall at such time or times and from time to time as they or he shall think fit but nevertheless as soon after my death as circumstances will permit having regard to the amount of my residuary estate at my death and the possibilities of sale and realization thereof and having regard also to the directions hereinbefore contained with respect to such sale and realization set apart and appropriate out of the residue of the monies to arise from such sale and realization a sum or sums amounting as nearly as may be in the whole to but not exceeding the sum of £1,000,000 sterling such sum or sums to be held upon the trusts hereinafter declared concerning the same.

30.—I DECLARE that my General Trustees or Trustee shall stand possessed of the said sum or sums amounting as nearly as may be in the whole to but not exceeding the sum of £1,000,000 sterling hereinbefore directed to be set apart and appropriated out of the said residuary monies to arise from the sale calling in and conversion of my residuary real and personal estate or to be provided by means of the accumulation hereinbefore directed upon trust to pay over the same to the following persons (namely) the Right Honourable and Right Reverend Arthur Foley Winnington-Ingram D.D. Lord Bishop of London the Right Reverend Cosmo Gordon Lang M.A. Bishop Suffragan of Stepney The Right Honorable Charles Henry Mills Baron Hillingdon the Right Honourable William Mansfield

Baron Sandhurst G.C.I.E. Walpole Greenwell of 2 Finch Lane in the City of London Esquire (now Sir Walpole Greenwell Bart.) William Edward Gillett of 5 Berners Street in the County of London Solicitor and my said sons William Whiteley and Frank Ernest Whiteley or the survivors or survivor of them and who and also any additional Trustees or Trustee to be appointed as next hereinafter mentioned and the survivors and survivor of them and the executors or administrators of such survivor are hereinafter referred to as "The Whiteley Homes Trustees" Provided always and I hereby declare that it shall be lawful for the said Walpole Greenwell and William Edward Gillett and for the survivor of them at any time or times after my death by deed to appoint any one or more person or persons (but not exceeding three altogether) to be an additional Trustee or additional Trustees together with the Whiteley Homes Trustees hereinbefore named for the purposes of the trusts next hereinafter declared And further that when such three additional Whiteley Homes Trustees shall have been so appointed it shall be lawful for the general body of the Whiteley Homes Trustees by deed to appoint any such other person or persons (without restriction as to number) to be an additional Trustee or additional Trustees for the purposes of the same trusts as the Whiteley Homes Trustees for the time being shall think fit AND I DECLARE that the receipt of the Whiteley Homes Trustees shall be an effectual discharge to my General Trustees or Trustee for the said sum or sums amounting as nearly as may be in the whole to but not exceeding £1,000,000 sterling AND I DECLARE that the Whiteley Homes Trustees shall stand possessed of the said sum or sums amounting as nearly as may be in the whole to but not exceeding the sum of £1,000,000 sterling so to be paid to them as aforesaid (hereinafter referred to as "the said trust legacy of £1,000,000") upon the trusts and subject to the powers and provisions hereinafter expressed and declared concerning the same Provided always and I declare that in case the monies paid by my General Trustees or Trustee to the Whiteley Homes Trustees under the trust or provision in that behalf hereinbefore contained shall not amount in the whole to the sum of £1,000,000 sterling then it shall be lawful for but not obligatory upon the Whiteley Homes Trustees in their absolute discretion for the purpose of making up the said trust legacy to the full amount of £1,000,000 sterling during such period or periods after my death as the Whiteley Homes Trustees shall think fit but not in any case for a longer period than 21 years from my death to accumulate the annual income of all or any part of the monies so paid to the Whiteley Homes Trustees as aforesaid or of any investments for the time being representing the same at compound interest by investing the same and the resulting income thereof in any of the modes of investment hereinafter authorised and any accumulations made as aforesaid may at any time be added to and dealt with and disposed of in like manner as the monies or investments from the investment of the income whereof such

3

accumulations shall have arisen so that the proceeds of the sale and conversion thereof may form part of and be added to the said trust legacy of £1,000,000 whereof trusts are next hereinafter declared.

31.—The Whiteley Homes Trustees shall stand possessed of the said trust legacy of £1,000,000 upon the trusts and subject to the powers and provisions following (that is to say) Upon trust from time to time to lay out a sufficient part or sufficient parts of the said trust legacy of £1,000,000 in the purchase of lands of freehold tenure situate in some or one of the Western Suburbs of London or in the adjacent country and if possible and convenient within 10 miles of Charing Cross and to be selected by the Whiteley Homes Trustees as a site for the erection thereon of buildings to be used and occupied as homes for aged poor persons and to be called " Whitely Homes for the Aged Poor " or by such other name or names as the Whiteley Homes Trustees shall in their discretion think fit but so that the name of " Whiteley " shall form part of such name or names And I declare it to be my wish that the site to be selected by the Whiteley Homes Trustees for the said Homes shall be in as bright cheerful and healthy spot as possible even if such a site can only be acquired at additional expense and that in selecting such site the Whiteley Homes Trustees shall so far as may be avoid a heavy clay soil and choose a soil of gravel sand or chalk And I empower my General Trustees or Trustee at the expense of my residuary estate to make or concur with the Whiteley Homes Trustees in making such application or applications from time to time or at any time to the High Court of Justice under the provisions in that behalf contained in the Mortmain and Charitable Uses Act 1891 or otherwise as may be necessary or expedient in order to obtain the sanction of the Court to the purchase or acquisition and retention of land to be used as a site for the erection of buildings to be used or occupied for the purposes aforesaid.

32.—I declare that the Whiteley Homes Trustees shall lay out a further sufficient part or further sufficient parts of the said trust legacy of £1,000,000 in the erection on the lands so to be purchased or acquired as aforesaid of buildings to be used and occupied by aged poor persons of either sex as Homes in their old age under and subject to such regulations and provisions as are hereinafter contained.

33.—I declare that for the purpose of purchasing the said lands and erection of the said buildings thereon the Whiteley Homes Trustees may expend such sum or sums of money and enter into such contracts or arrangements with any person or persons and engage and employ such architects builders contractors surveyors workmen and agents at such remuneration salaries and wages as they may from time to time think fit and may also from time to time alter rescind or vary such contracts or arrangements in any manner

4

they may think proper with power at any time to discharge remove or dismiss any such architects builders contractors surveyors workmen and agents or any of them at pleasure And I declare it to be my wish that the buildings to be erected for the said Homes shall be of good and substantial character and of a plain and useful design and shall be well lighted ventilated and drained and so placed as to be protected as far as possible from the north and east winds and to be open to the south and west and that an outdoor shelter shall be provided as part of the said buildings.

34.—I declare that the Whiteley Homes Trustees shall stand seized and possessed of the said lands so to be purchased and acquired as aforesaid and the buildings erected thereon Upon trust to permit the same to be used and occupied by aged poor persons of either sex as homes under and subject to the provisions and regulations hereinafter contained and either rent free or at such rent or rents either generally or in any particular case or cases as the Whiteley Homes Trustees shall think proper to require as necessary or desirable in order to provide a fund for or towards the repair and upkeep of the said Homes or otherwise to carry into effect the general objects of the trusts intended to be hereby created in regard to the said Homes.

35.—I declare that all rents (if any) which shall be received by the Whiteley Homes Trustees in respect of the said buildings shall be applied by them (together with any monies applicable under the trusts of this my Will for the same purpose) in or towards payment of the rates taxes and other outgoings payable in respect of the said buildings or in or towards the repair and upkeep of the same or otherwise generally towards the purposes of the trusts intended to be hereby created in regard to the said Homes.

36.—I declare that the Whiteley Homes Trustees shall stand possessed of all such part or parts of the said trust legacy of £1,000,000 as shall not be applied in the purchase of the said lands and in the erection of the buildings thereon upon trust from time to time to invest the same in the names of the Whiteley Homes Trustees in some or one of the modes of investment hereinafter authorised with power from time to time to vary such investments into or for any others of a like nature And upon trust from time to time to apply the dividends and income arising from the said investments for or towards any of the following objects or purposes that is to say (1) The payment of all rates and taxes and other outgoings payable in respect of the said Homes (2) The repairs and insurance of the said Homes in such manner as the Whiteley Homes Trustees shall think fit (3) The giving of pecuniary assistance or relief temporary or permanent to any inmate or inmates for the time being of the said Homes (4) In any other manner or for or towards any other object

5

or purpose which shall in the opinion of the Whiteley Homes Trustees conduce to or enhance the utility and advantage of the said Homes and the benefits and advantages intended to be conferred on the inmates thereof (5) And in particular I recommend the Whiteley Homes Trustees on Michaelmas Day in every year to make some small gift (pecuniary or otherwise) to each inmate of the said Homes that day being my birthday.

37.—The persons qualified to be admitted as inmates of the said Homes shall be persons of good character and of sound mind and not affected by any infectious or contagious disease and not having been convicted of any criminal offence and being male of not less than 65 years and being female of not less than 60 years of age And it is my desire that in the selection of inmates of the said Homes a preference shall be given to persons or the wives of persons who have been engaged in commercial or agricultural pursuits.

38.—The Whiteley Homes Trustees shall have full and absolute discretion as to determining the name by which the said Homes shall be called or known (but so that the name of "Whiteley" shall form part of such name) the time and manner of election of the first inmates of the said Homes and the duration of the residence of any inmate therein (the Whiteley Homes Trustees being expressly empowered and authorised to discharge and remove any such inmate in their discretion without assigning any reason for the exercise of such discretion) and generally as to all matters and questions arising with respect to the conduct and management of the said Homes but subject to the exercise of such discretion they shall as soon as conveniently may be after my death frame general rules and regulations for the management and conduct of the said Homes and generally for the administration of the trusts by this my Will declared for the establishment and maintenance thereof and the time manner and conditions of election and discharge of inmates thereof as to all which matters and all other matters and questions I declare that the Whiteley Homes Trustees shall have full and absolute discretion.

39.—I DECLARE that all monies which under any of the trusts in this my Will declared are liable to be invested may be invested by the Trustees or Trustee whose duty it is to invest the same in any of the following modes of investment (that is to say) in any of the public stocks or funds or Government securities of the United Kingdom or India or any British Colony or Dependency or any securities the interest on which is or shall be guaranteed by Parliament or upon freehold copyhold leasehold or chattel real securities in Great Britain but not in Ireland or in Stock of the Bank of England or of the Bank of Ireland or Metropolitan Stock or London County Council Stock or in or upon the Debentures Debenture Stock or guaranteed or preference or ordinary stock or shares of any railway or other

6

Company a fixed or minimum rate of interest or dividend on which is guaranteed (whether absolutely or otherwise) by the Government of India or in or upon the Debentures or debenture or rent charge stock of any railway canal dock harbour gas water or other Company incorporated by special Act of the Imperial Parliament or of the legislature of any British Colony or Dependency or by Royal Charter or in or upon the guaranteed or preference stock or shares of any such company as aforesaid which shall have paid dividends upon its ordinary capital at the rate of at least 3 per cent. per annum for at least five years prior to the time of investment of which fact a letter purporting to be signed by the Secretary of the Company or by a Banker or a member of a firm of Bankers or by the Secretary or Manager of a Joint Stock Bank or of any branch thereof shall be sufficient evidence or in or upon the stocks bonds debentures or securities of any Municipality Company or District Council Public Body or Local Authority in the United Kingdom but not in any stocks funds bonds shares or securities to bearer or transferable by mere delivery or delivery and endorsement though coming within the general description of investments hereinbefore authorised.

41.—I AUTHORISE my General Trustees or Trustee in substitution for the power in that behalf conferred on personal representatives by the Land Transfer Act 1897 at their or his discretion (and although they or any of them may be interested in the mode or result of such appropriation) to appropriate any part of my estate real or personal hereinbefore devised and bequeathed to my General Trustees in trust for sale and conversion in its then actual condition or state of investment in or towards satisfaction of any legacy or share of residue hereinbefore bequeathed out of or in the trust estate with power for that purpose conclusively to determine the value of the said trust estate or any part or parts thereof in any manner they or he shall think fit And I declare that any property appropriated under the power last hereinbefore contained in or towards satisfaction of any legacy or share not absolutely vested in possession and immediately payable or transferable shall notwithstanding such appropriation remain subject to the trusts and powers hereinbefore declared and contained concerning my said estate hereinbefore devised or bequeathed in trust as aforesaid or such of the same trusts and powers as may be applicable thereto in the same manner as if no such appropriation had been made.

43.—I DECLARE that in addition to the ordinary indemnity and right to reimbursement by law given to Trustees any Trustees or Trustee appointed under this my Will may dispense wholly or partially with the investigation or production of the lessor's title in lending money on leasehold securities or otherwise may accept less than a marketable title without being answerable for loss occasioned thereby and may determine all questions and matters of doubt

7

arising in such of the trusts of this my Will as are hereby reposed in such Trustees or Trustee respectively and every such determination whether made upon a question actually raised or implied in the acts or proceedings of the said Trustees or Trustee shall be conclusive and binding on all persons interested under the trusts of this my Will or any Codicil hereto.

44.—I DECLARE that my Executors or Executor or any Trustees or Trustee for the time being of this my Will acting in any of the general trusts thereof or in any of the special trusts hereinbefore declared shall not be bound in any case to act personally but shall be at full liberty to employ and to pay out of any trust funds coming to their or his hands a Solicitor or any other Agent to transact all or any business of whatsoever nature required to be done in the premises including the receipt and payment of money and shall not be responsible for any default of such Solicitor or Agent or for any loss occasioned by his employment And I further declare that any Executor or Trustee for the time being of this my Will who shall be a Solicitor or other person engaged in any profession or business shall be entitled to charge and be paid all usual professional or other charges for any business done by him or any partner of his in the execution of or in connection with the Executorship or the trusts of which he shall as a Trustee whether in the ordinary course of his business or not and although not of a nature requiring the employment of a Solicitor or other professional person.

46.—I HEREBY DECLARE that if and so often as the said Trustees hereby constituted (of whatever class the same may be) shall die in my lifetime or if such Trustees or any of them or any Trustees or Trustee appointed under this present power or any other power contained in this my Will or by a Court of competent jurisdiction shall die after my decease or remain out of the United Kingdom for more than twelve calendar months or shall desire to be discharged or refuse or become incapable to act it shall be lawful for the surviving or continuing Trustees or Trustee of the class in which such vacancy or disqualification shall occur (and for this purpose every refusing or retiring Trustee shall if willing to act in the execution of this power be considered a continuing Trustee) or for the acting Executors or Executor Administrators or Administrator of the last surviving or continuing Trustee of the same class to appoint a new Trustee or new Trustees in the place of the Trustee or Trustees so dying or remaining out of the United Kingdom or desiring to be discharged or refusing or becoming unfit or incapable to act as aforesaid And upon every such appointment the number of Trustees may be increased or (subject to the proviso next hereinafter contained) be reduced but not to less than two Provided nevertheless and it is my wish that the number of the Whiteley Homes Trustees shall at all times be kept up to no less than nine and that in the event of the number of such Trustees becoming at any time reduced

8

below nine the vacancy or vacancies shall as soon as circumstances will conveniently admit be filled up so as to restore that number but nevertheless any acts or proceedings of the Whiteley Homes Trustees for the time being in the interval before the filling up of such vacancy or vacancies shall not be invalidated by reason of the same not having been done.

47.—I DECLARE that upon any appointment of a new Trustee or new Trustees the trust property (if any) then vested in the Trustees or Trustee of the class in which such vacancy or disqualification shall occur or in the heirs executors or administrators of the last survivor of such Trustees shall as soon as circumstances will admit be vested in the Trustees for the time being of the same class but every new Trustee may as well before as after the trust property shall have been so transferred execute all the trusts and powers in respect of which trusts or powers he shall be so appointed a Trustee as fully and effectually as if he had been by this my Will constituted a Trustee.

Appendix B

A LIST OF THE TRUSTEES OF THE WHITELEY HOMES UP TO THE END OF 1971

(Those whose names are in bold type constituted the Board in 1971)

ORIGINAL TRUSTEES (Appointed in Clause 36 of Mr Whiteley's Will)

The Right Honourable and Right Reverend Arthur Foley WINNINGTON-INGRAM, PC KCVO DD
        Lord Bishop of London
        First Chairman until his death on 26 May 1946

The Right Reverend Cosmo Gordon LANG, MA
        Bishop Suffragan of Stepney
        Retired from Trusteeship on preferment to the Archbishopric of York in 1908
                        (Deed dated 2 June 1909)

The Right Honourable Charles Henry MILLS
        Baron Hillingdon
        Retired from Trusteeship in 1909   (Deed dated 2 June 1909)

The Right Honourable William MANSFIELD, GCIE GCSI PC
        Baron Sandhurst
        Retired from Trusteeship on appointment to the Office of Lord Chamberlain
                       (Deed dated 19 June 1912)

Sir Walpole GREENWELL Bt
        Died 29 October 1919

William Edward GILLETT
        Solicitor
        Died 7 March 1927

William WHITELEY
        Son of the Testator
        Died in 1937

Frank Ernest WHITELEY
        Son of the Testator
        Died 19 November 1929

ADDITIONAL (ORIGINAL) TRUSTEES (Appointed under the power conferred in Clause 36 of Mr Whiteley's Will upon Sir Walpole Greenwell and William Edward Gillett by Deed of Appointment dated 2 June 1909)

Colonel The Honourable Arthur Grenville BRODRICK, TD DL
        Died 18 September 1934

Colonel Sir Edward Willis Duncan WARD, KCB KCVO
        Permanent Under-Secretary of State for War
        Retired from Trusteeship   (Deed dated 2 February 1920)

Sir Edward Feetham COATES, Bt
        Member of Parliament
        Died 14 August 1921

ADDITIONAL TRUSTEES (Appointed by the existing Board of Trustees under the power conferred
upon them in Clause 36 of Mr Whiteley's Will)

Henry Luke PAGET   (Deed dated 2 June 1909)
        Bishop Suffragan of Stepney
        Retired from Trusteeship on preferment to the Bishopric of Chester
                                                (Deed dated 2 February 1920)

Sir Arthur Sackville Trevor GRIFFITH BOSCAWEN, PC MP
        Died 1 June 1946   (Deed dated 19 June 1912)

Henry MOSLEY   (Deed dated 2 February 1920)
        Bishop Suffragan of Stepney
        Retired from Trusteeship   (Deed dated 19 March 1929)

William Hayes FISHER   (Deed dated 2 February 1920)
        Baron Downham of Fulham
        Died 2 July 1920

Colonel Sir Courtauld THOMSON, KBE CB   (Deed dated 2 February 1920)
        (later created Baron Courtauld Thomson)
        Died 1 November 1954

Sir Bernard Eyre GREENWELL, Bt   (Deed dated 2 February 1920)
        (son of Sir Walpole Greenwell)
        Died in December 1939

Herbert Pike PEASE, PC MP   (Deed dated 31 December 1920)
        (later created Baron Daryngton of Witley)
        Died 10 May 1949

Dorothy EGERTON, OBE JP   (Deed dated 31 December 1920)
        Died 2 August 1959

Sir George Stapylton BARNES, KCB KCSI   (Deed dated 12 June 1922)
        Retired from Trusteeship in March 1944

Howard WILLIAMS   (Deed dated 12 June 1922)
        Died 9 January 1929

Laura Helen POLLOCK   (Deed dated 20 October 1924)
        (later the Dowager Viscountess Hanworth)
        Retired from Trusteeship in December 1941

Colonel William Alan GILLETT   (Deed dated 11 July 1925)
      (son of William Edward Gillett)
      Knighted 1 April 1949
      Died 18 February 1959

Charles Edward CURZON   (Deed dated 19 March 1929)
      Bishop Suffragan of Stepney
      Retired from Trusteeship in 1936 on preferment to the Bishopric of Exeter

John Victor McMILLAN   (Deed dated 25 February 1939)
      Lord Bishop of Guildford
      Appointed Second Chairman 22 February 1946
      Retired from Chairmanship in June 1954
      Died 15 August 1956

Sir Walter Stewart HOWARD, MBE BA DL JP   (Deed dated 25 February 1939)
      Appointed Third Chairman 30 June 1956
      Retired from Chairmanship 5 December 1961
      Retired from Trusteeship (Deed dated 9 July 1975)
      Appointed Trustee Emeritus from 28 January 1975
      Resigned as Trustee Emeritus 17 July 1981

Isolda Rosamond Viscountess HANWORTH, JP   (Deed dated 30 March 1948)

Frank MAYNELL, CBE JP   (Deed dated 30 March 1945)
      Appointed Fourth Chairman 5 December 1961
      Died 12 November 1964

John Henry WENHAM, JP   (Deed dated 3 June 1950)
      Knighted in June 1954
      Retired from Trusteeship 10 October 1961

Bridget Baroness SOMERLEYTON   (Deed dated 3rd June 1950)
      (later the Dowager Lady Somerleyton)
      Retired from Trusteeship 26 May 1981

Honor Dorothea BARNES   (Deed dated 9 December 1954)
      Retired from Trusteeship 3 July 1979

The Right Reverend Henry Colville Montgomery CAMPBELL, MC DD
                                  (Deed dated 9 December 1954)
      Lord Bishop of Guildford
      Later Lord Bishop of London
      Retired from Trusteeship 18 September 1962

Dorothy Mabel COMBE   (Deed dated 25 February 1939)
      Retired from Trusteeship

Major The Honourable Frances Stewart MACKENZIE   (Deed dated 25 February 1939)
      (nephew of Colonel the Hon. A. G. Brodrick)
      Killed in action in1943

Edward Shaw HOSE, CMG   (Deed dated 25 February 1939)
     Died 12 September 1946

Major Graham Hamilton GREENWELL, MC   (Deed dated 9 September 1940)
     Retired from Trusteeship   (Deed dated 21 April 1949)

Dr. Geoffrey Reynolds Yonge RADCLIFFE   (Deed dated 11 April 1949)
     Died 18 July 1959

Sybilla Jane BAILEY   (Deed dated 11 April 1945)
     Retired from Trusteeship   (Deed dated 30 March 1948)

Anthony Charles BARNES, DSO OBE   (Deed dated 30 March 1948)
     (son of Sir George Barnes)
     Died 11 September 1974

Douglas Eric Baron HACKING, MA   (Deed dated 9 December 1954)
     Solicitor
     Appointed Fifth Chairman 26 January 1964
     Died 7 November 1971

Basil William Sholto MACKENZIE, MD FRCP   (Deed dated 25 October 1956)
     Baron Amulree
     Retired from Trusteeship   (Deed dated 18 March 1976)

Charles Henry Christian COMBE   (Deed dated 23 November 1959)
     (son of Mrs. D. M. Combe)
     Retired from Trusteeship   (Deed dated 7 November 1967)

Dr. Margaret Joan SUTTILL, MB BS   (Deed dated 23 November 1959)
     Retired from Trusteeship 22 April 1968

Elisabeth Venetia Marian BRODRICK   (Deed dated 31 January 1963)
     (daughter of Colonel The Honourable A. G. Brodrick)

Major Robert Asgill COLVILLE, TD   (Deed dated 31 January 1963)
     Retired from Trusteeship October 1977 (Deed dated 5 June 1978)

Group Captain Frank WHITWORTH, QC   (Deed dated 31 January 1963)

The Honourable Elizabeth Anne HAYTOR, JP (Deed dated 21 April 1969)
     Retired from Trusteeship 17 July 1980 (Deed dated 13 October 1980)

Michael Alan FISHER, FCA   (Deed dated 21 April 1969)

Appendix C

In the High Court of Justice.

CHANCERY DIVISION.

ROYAL COURTS OF JUSTICE,
Wednesday, 23rd February, 1910.

BEFORE
Mr. JUSTICE EVE.

In Re William Whiteley, deceased.

THE BISHOP OF LONDON and Others
—*v.*—
WHITELEY and Others.

[*Transcript from the Shorthand Notes of* H. H. TOLCHER & Co., 93 & 94, *Chancery Lane, and* CORFIELD & HERSEE, 22, *Chancery Lane, W.C.*]

JUDGMENT on ADJOURNED SUMMONS.

Mr. Justice EVE : Of the two questions raised upon this Summons the one involves only the construction of a particular Will ; the other relates to a matter of more general importance. By the first question the Court is asked to determine whether, according to the true construction of the testator's Will, the Homes, for the erection and maintenance of which the testator so generously provided, must be erected on a single site, or whether it is open to the trustees at their discretion to select, within the limits imposed by the testator, more than one site for such erection ?

In approaching the consideration of this question the magnitude of the bequest, and the improbability (which the testator himself appreciated) of the whole sum being available at one and the same moment of time for payment to the trustees, must not be lost sight of, nor must the wish and intention of the testator—obvious throughout his Will—that his benefactions of a public character should be permanently and prominently associated with his name, be disregarded.

I think it is impossible to read the Will without coming to the conclusion that the testator was a man of strong individuality, the nature of whose charitable dispositions was, in part, determined by his wish therewith to identify his personality, and thereby to perpetuate his memory.

Bearing these matters in mind, and turning now to the clauses of the Will dealing with the particular bequest under consideration, I think the use of such phrases as "from time to time," and "name or names," each occurring twice in Clause 31, and of the word "lands" in the plural in Clauses 31, 32, and 33, is consistent with either view urged before me. As I have pointed out, the testator contemplated that the bequest would probably be satisfied by periodical payments, and, apart from this, even if the whole legacy had been paid over in one sum, no one would expect the trustees to acquire by one purchase, or at one time, the whole of the land required for the trust—considerations which, in my opinion, are amply sufficient to account for the use of the expression "from time to time," and of the word "lands" and not "land." The alternative "name or names" is discounted by the use of the singular "name" in Clause 38, where the question of nomenclature is particularly dealt with, and even as an alternative would not be inappropriately applied to a single aggregation of Homes, some used for male and others for female inmates.

Treating the expressions with which I have now dealt as ambiguous in the sense that they are not necessarily confined to either alternative,

the majority of the trustees who advocate what I may call the distributive construction, are forced to rely on the direction that the lands to be purchased are to be "situate in some or one of the western suburbs of London or in the adjacent country," as establishing their contention. I say this, because, in my opinion, all that follows in the Will relating to this trust is more indicative of a single site than of a multiplicity of sites. Am I justified in holding, as a matter of construction, that these indications are controlled by the direction above referred to ? On the whole, I do not think that I am, and very largely for this reason—that the testator directs the purchase of lands in some or one of the western suburbs, or in the adjacent country, to be made as "a site" for the Homes—not, be it observed, as "a site or sites," but as a site for that which, I believe, he contemplated should be a conspicuous and concentrated memorial of his charity. It may be that the word "or" has inadvertently crept in between the words "some" and "one" in the direction, but, construing the phrase as it stands, I think it may well be that it was used in order not to tie the hands of the trustees within too restricted limits, and to leave them free, so long as the Homes are situated in the western suburbs, to disregard the exact physical boundaries of any particular suburb.

I hold, therefore, that the trustees are not entitled to select more than one site for the Homes, and I do not accede to the suggestion that such a construction involves the erection of a gigantic and inhospitable institution. It is, in my opinion, quite consistent with the laying out of an attractive and cheerful aggregation of houses wholly suitable for the purposes contemplated by the testator.

The second question in the summons raised the point whether, in matters relating to the administration of the trust, a majority of the trustees has power to bind the minority ? By Clause 38 of the Will, a very wide discretion is vested in the trustees, not only upon all matters relating to the management and conduct of the Homes, but also upon all other matters and questions affecting the trust, and by Clause 46 the testator fixes the minimum number of trustees at nine. On behalf of the applicants, it is urged that unanimity in such a body upon all matters of detail is unattainable, and that the Courts have long since recognised this fact, and in order to facilitate administration, and avoid the expense and delay of frequent applications for their intervention, have laid down a rule that, in the administration of a public trust, the act of the majority of the trustees is to be treated as the act of the whole body. In support of this proposition the cases of Wilkinson v. Malin, 2, Tyrwhitt, 544 ; and Perry v. Shipway, 1, Giffard, are cited and relied upon.

The Respondents do not dispute the existence of the rule, but maintain that its applicability is limited to cases in which the act of the body is an act in which the public, or the particular members of the public affected by the trust, have a direct interest ; for example, the appointment of a minister or a schoolmaster ; that is to say, the appointment of a person to discharge the duties of an office, the proper discharge of which is a matter of direct interest to that part of the public which is represented, in the one case, by the congregation, and, in the other, by those who are entitled to the educational benefits of the school. They deny that the rule has any application to matters of administrative detail, and assert that there is no authority for holding that it has. It is true that the authorities referred to by the Applicants are each concerned with the appointment of a person to discharge the duties of an office of a public nature, but I cannot read the observations of Lord Lyndhurst, at page 571 of 2nd Tyrwhitt, as limiting the principle there stated to the particular class of case with which he was there dealing ; and I think, when he speaks of "a trust of a public nature," he is using an expression equivalent, for all practical purposes, to "a trust of a charitable nature." In other words I regard the words "public" and "charitable" in this connection as synonymous ; and, so regarding them,

I think that the rule on which the Applicants rely is of general application, and that I ought to answer the second question (omitting the words "or sites") in the affirmative. The costs of all parties will be taxed as between solicitor and client and paid out of the trust legacy.

Mr. BUCKMASTER : I suppose, my Lord, the usual order as to costs will be made ?

Mr. Justice EVE : Yes.

Mr. BUCKMASTER : May I just say one word upon that, my Lord ? Your Lordship, of course, has realised that there have been some unusual expenses incurred on both sides in this case, and my clients are willing, if your Lordship sees fit to approve, that those unusual expenses should be borne by this million fund. Perhaps your Lordship would allow that to be done as an exceptional matter ?

Mr. Justice EVE : What is the nature of the unusual expenses, Mr. Buckmaster.

Mr. BUCKMASTER : The presence of myself and my learned friend Mr. Younger, chiefly, my Lord.

Mr. Justice EVE : That is an appeal to my personal sense of charity.

Mr. BUCKMASTER : What I mean is this. I am not, of course, saying that other services might not have been rendered quite as efficiently, but the point is this. The matter is a very important one with regard to the construction of the Will, and the directions to be given as to this vast charity, and the question whether the trustees were right or wrong.

Mr. Justice EVE : They would not be included, I suppose, in the ordinary solicitor and client taxation ?

Mr. BUCKMASTER : Simply with that direction, I doubt if they would. Both sides agree, I think.

Mr. Justice EVE : What does Mr. Lawrence say ?

Mr. P. O. LAWRENCE : I certainly leave it to your Lordship.

Mr. Justice EVE : This is a very rich man's estate.

Mr. P. O. LAWRENCE : Yes, my Lord, and I certainly would support my friend if your Lordship could see your way to do it.

Mr. Justice EVE : Very well. I think the magnitude of the sum involved will justify it.

Mr. BUCKMASTER : If your Lordship pleases.

Appendix D

Financial Statement 28ᵗʰ February 1910

Amount received from Executors and Trustees of William Whiteley	£840000 . .	
Interest and Dividends received		
Interest on Deposit	4499 8 5	
Dividends on		
Consols	2015 15 2	
Transvaal Stock	1.716 3 9	
Irish Land Stock	453 3 7	
Metropolitan Water Board Stock	1.414 11 8	
		5599 14 2
	£10.099 2 7	
Balance on Deposit account	500.272 18 1	
Balance on Current account	2330 1 .	
	£502.602 19 1	

	Nominal value	Cost
Amount Invested	£355.000 . .	£347.152 8 11 .

134

In the High Court of Justice.

CHANCERY DIVISION

ROYAL COURTS OF JUSTICE,
Wednesday, 15th February, 1911.

BEFORE
MR. JUSTICE EVE.

In re WILLIAM WHITELEY, deceased.

THE BISHOP OF LONDON and Others

—v.—

WHITELEY and Others.

[*Transcript from the Shorthand Notes of* H. H. TOLCHER & Co., 93 & 94, *Chancery Lane, W.C., and* CORFIELD & HEISER, 22, *Chancery Lane. W.C.*]

JUDGMENT on ADJOURNED SUMMONS.

Mr. Justice EVE: If this were a matter upon which I am called upon to exercise my discretion, I have no doubt whatever I should adopt the view the Trustees themselves have adopted that this is far and away the most eligible of the sites which have been offered to them, but that is not my province. My province is to construe the Will of the testator, and, in so far as I am able, to arrive at a conclusion as to what he meant.

The whole point really lies upon the construction of the few words which have been read more than once in the course of Mr. Lawrence's argument, but which I will now read once more. The Trustees are to stand possessed of the legacy which I am glad to hear does in fact amount to the full sum of £1,000,000 " upon trust from time to time to lay out a sufficient part or sufficient parts of the said trust legacy of £1,000,000 in the purchase of lands of freehold tenure situate in or in the country adjacent to some or one of the Western Suburbs of London." The first point of construction I have to determine on looking at the Will is, do the words " in the adjacent country " refer to the immediately antecedent word " London " or do they refer to the words which precede the word " London," namely, " the Western Suburbs of London," in other words, am I to read it in one way or the other; am I to read it as though it were in the purchase of lands of freehold tenure situate in or in the country adjacent to some or one of the Western Suburbs of London, or am I to read it as in the purchase of lands of freehold tenure situate in some or one of the Western Suburbs of or in the country adjacent to London, I think that I am bound to read it in the first of those two alternatives. For some reason or other which it is not necessary to enquire into, and which if one enquired into, it might well be one could not ascertain, the testator chose to locate, as far as he could, the site of these homes in the Western Suburbs of London, and he realised and must have realised having regard to the magnitude of the bequest and the extent of land which would be required for the adequate administration of the charity, it might well be possible that sufficient land could not be obtained in any of the Western Suburbs, and he. therefore, thought it prudent to extend the area within which the site might be selected to, in my opinion, the country adjacent to those Western Suburbs. I think, therefore, upon the point as to whether the words " in the adjacent country " must be read as applicable to London or the various Western Suburbs of London, on the whole it is, I will not say

clear because I do not think many of the questions which have been submitted to me on this particular Will are perfectly clear, but I think it is preferable to hold they are applicable to the larger place. " Western Suburbs of London " and not merely to the word " London " alone.

That by no means disposes of the points that are taken by the Trustees. In the next place it is said Croydon, in the immediate neighbourhood of which lies the estate which the Trustees are desirous of acquiring, is in fact a Western Suburb of London, and that argument is supported by the contention that in determining what is a Western Suburb regard must be had not to the four points of the compass, but to only one other point. the eastern point, and if you draw a line north and south through a point which would represent the centre of what is now called the County of London, inasmuch as Croydon falls to the west of that line so drawn, it is right and proper to hold that Croydon is a Western Suburb. I do not think that that is a fair way of ascertaining what the testator means when he speaks of " The Western Suburbs." I think to a man like Mr. Whiteley, who was well acquainted with London, who was not only resident in London, but had depôts and branches of his business in all parts of the country surrounding London, it would have been more or less absurd to speak of London as divided, merely so far as its suburbs were concerned, by one line passing from north to south. I think to an ordinary Londoner you must in addition to that line draw another line at right angles to it, passing through some ascertained point, and that in considering the suburbs you must take it they are properly divided into four, answering to the four points of the compass. I am not deciding this point, because it may be that other matters should be taken into consideration, but my own view is for the purpose of ascertaining what is a Western Suburb within the meaning of this Will, the Trustees will be well advised to treat Charing Cross as the point at which the two lines would intersect at right angles and to treat so much of the Western part of London as would lie within an angle of 90 degrees drawn from that point as constituting the Western Suburb, and that I think is roughly what the testator meant, and included as the Western Suburbs. I do not think it would be right to say he excluded altogether the fact that there were Northern Suburbs and Southern Suburbs of London, and that he intended to treat as Western Suburbs all those which lie to the west of the one line. I think, therefore, so treating it, I cannot treat Croydon as a Western Suburb.

Then it is said even supposing that that view be taken there is still this construction open that Croydon is a part of the country or situate in a part of the country adjacent to a Western Suburb. I have not myself drawn the line to see whether any part of Croydon would be actually contiguous or adjoining to any suburb which would come within the 90 degrees which I have indicated, but I should think in all probability it would not. As far as I can see there would be other places which would intervene between the limits of any Western Suburb within that portion of the circle and Croydon, but as Mr. Lawrence has pointed out the word " adjacent " must be construed not as strictly as the word " adjoining," but as a word the construction of which is more or less regulated by the context in which you find it. In my view the word must be read in a limited sense. I do not think that the testator used it as though he were using it in connection with some charity or charitable institution which was to be for the benefit of a particular suburb and the country adjacent thereto. In that connection I think it is quite likely I should have felt that the word ought to be construed in the wider sense in which it was construed by the Privy Council in the case to which my attention has been called. I think the testator used it as intending a site which was to be as far as possible in the country near to, and as close as practicable to, the suburbs

3

in which primarily he desired the institution to be erected. So construing Feb. 15, 1911 — Judgment on Adjourned Summons. it I do not think I ought to hold that Croydon, which must, as I think, be separated by a considerable number of intervening localities lying outside the limits of the part of the circle I have indicated, can possibly be treated as lying in country adjacent to any Western Suburb of London.

For these reasons, and, if I may say so, not having heard Mr. Rolt on the whereabouts of the particular locality, I come to the conclusion I cannot sanction the trustees acquiring this particular site.

The rest of the Summons, I think, does not now become material except as regards the costs, and as this is a very proper and necessary question to be determined I must direct the costs of all parties, as between solicitor and client, to be taxed and paid out of the trust legacy.

Mr. P. O. LAWRENCE: Will your Lordship allow the cost of a shorthand note, and one copy of your Lordship's Judgment for the use of the Trustees?

Mr. Justice EVE: Yes.

Mr. P. O. LAWRENCE: Then, my Lord, there is one small point on the Summons which the Trustees are very anxious to have determined, and that is question 3, "If the said estate is not within the said area of selection then the directions of the Court as to the area open to the Whiteley Homes Trustees in selecting a site for the said Homes."

Mr. Justice EVE: I think I ought to say inasmuch as the contract is conditional, you have my authority if you wish to take the opinion of the Court of Appeal, to say it is a case in which the Court might advance the hearing of the Appeal.

Mr. P. O. LAWRENCE: I am pleased to say, my Lord, that I do not think the Trustees desire to do anything of the kind. Your Lordship has in your Judgment, for the Trustees' guidance, mentioned two of the lines, and we have a map in which a line intersects at right angles Charing Cross, but there is this difficulty that even if we chose the Hillingdon site it is well within the radius, and then comes the question what is a suburb of London, and whether "the adjacent country" extends 18 miles from Charing Cross. Your Lordship sees if you take Uxbridge, which is connected with London by trams, it is 17 or 18 miles from Charing Cross.

Mr. Justice EVE: And not in the County of London, I suppose?

Mr. P. O. LAWRENCE: Uxbridge is not within the County of London, but it is in the County of Middlesex. We do not want to enter into contracts with people until we know what we can do.

Mr. Justice EVE: Certainly not. If you take the centre of Charing Cross and take an angle of 45 degrees above the intersecting line, and pursue those lines, that would include Uxbridge?

Mr. P. O. LAWRENCE: Yes, easily. Now the question comes upon the other point of distance. We have your Lordship's definition of the two lines outside, but we do not want it afterwards urged that Uxbridge is not a suburb, and is not country adjacent to a suburb. The difficulty is what is the real definition of "suburb." We have the Western Suburb defined by your Lordship, and we have the line quite clearly defined on a map which goes to some 20 or 30 miles outside.

Mr. Justice EVE: Is there any objection to saying that all within the London postal area is suburb, and that part of the country is country adjoining a suburb?

Mr. P. O. LAWRENCE: I am afraid that leaves them in a doubt as to how far they can go outside the postal district. The postal district, I am told, goes to Hanwell, which is in the direction of Uxbridge, but that falls short of Uxbridge by some six or seven miles.

Mr. Justice EVE: I did not mean to say anything that is adjacent must be adjoining. If you wish my opinion as regards Uxbridge I should have thought it would be country adjacent to a western suburb.

Mr. P. O. LAWRENCE: If your Lordship says that, that is a guide for the Trustees. I do not say they will confine themselves to Uxbridge

4

Feb. 15, 1911. — Judgment on Adjourned Summons.

without considering it again. I do not know if my learned friend Mr. Rolt would have anything to say to that. I should like it determined now as we do not want to bring another summons before the Court with regard to this matter.

Mr. ROLT: So far as I know I do not think there is any doubt that Uxbridge is a suburb. I should have thought the idea of suburb was a town which was joined on to London by other towns, that is to say, there was no country intervening, and it is not necessary for it to be within the postal district. Croydon is not in the postal district, but nobody suggests it is not a suburb.

Mr. SARGANT: My Lord, may I suggest that they may go out a good deal more than 10 miles. The testator says you had better be within 10 miles if you can, and I should have thought that would take them at least as far as Uxbridge.

Mr. P. O. LAWRENCE: Even the Attorney General appears to be of opinion that the Uxbridge site would be within the terms of the Will. Perhaps we might leave it without your Lordship making any definite order.

Mr. Justice EVE: Yes.

Mr. P. O. LAWRENCE: Your Lordship has already said we might have a transcript of your Lordship's Judgment, and might we have a transcript also of this discussion, as we think it might be a guide to the trustees?

Mr. Justice EVE: Certainly.

Appendix F

AGREED TERMS OF THE EMPLOYMENT BY THE WHITELEY HOMES TRUST OF MR. WALTER CAVE AS CONSULTING ARCHITECT

Annual Retaining fee £750

1. To attend when required at Meetings of the Trustees, and generally to advise them on Architectural matters.

2. Advice as to regulating Competitions and drawing up the Conditions.

3. Assisting the Trustees in assessing the Competitions.

4. Assisting the Trustees as to the drawing up of Contracts with Builders etc..

5. General advice as to Fencing, Roads, Sewers and Lighting.

6. Interviewing Local Authorities in relation to the Scheme as far as it affects the buildings and roads, but not to include any plans which may be required by them.

7. Countersigning all Certificates.

8. The Consulting Architect shall not take part in any Competitions but nothing in the terms of his appointment shall prevent him acting as Architect for any part of the proposed work on behalf of the Trustees.

9. The retaining fee not to include out of pocket and travelling expenses.

10. In the event of Mr Cave being employed either as sole or joint Constructing Architect of any block of the new buildings and his duties covered by the retaining fee becoming in consequence wholly or in part merged in his duties as such Constructing Architect he being paid for such last mentioned duties by commission on the ordinary scale according to the Royal Institute of British Architects then his retaining fee shall be reduced to such extent as may be fair and proper. Such reduction to be agreed upon between the Trustees and Mr Cave and in the event of dispute by arbitration in a manner directed by the President of the R.I.B.A.

11. If not employed either as sole or joint Architect a fee of ½% on all Contracts for buildings designed by others, such fee to be in consideration of superintendence of such buildings on behalf of the Trustees. This is in addition to the usual charges of the R.I.B.A. payable to the Architects of these buildings. All Certificates issued by such Architects to be countersigned by the Consulting Architect if required by the Trustees.

12. A copy of all plans of buildings, roads, drains, etc., to be deposited with the Consulting Architect on behalf of the Trustees.

13. The Consulting Architect if required by the Trustees to compile from all these plans etc., a complete Block Plan of the whole Estate, shewing all sewers, and drains, and runs of the telephone, electric mains, and positions of all buildings etc.. These plans to become the property of the Trustees and to be paid for by an agreed fee and in case of difference to be decided by arbitration.

14. A suitable office and sanitary convenience to be erected on the Site for the use of the Consulting Architect. The installation of a telephone to same if reasonably practicable.

15. The Consulting Architect to have control subject to the consent of the Trustees of the disposal of all surplus material on the Site, carting, stacking materials, temporary fencing, position of Latrines and Notice Boards etc..

16. The Consulting Architect to have control subject to the consent of the Trustees over the appointment and duties of the Clerk of the Works.

17. The appointment of Consulting Architect to be for three years terminable by six months notice during that period on either side.

18. General arbitration clause.

19. The duties of the Consulting Architect NOT to include:

(1) Responsibility for any electrical work or engineering work for which an Engineer should be employed.

(2) Responsibility for any road making, for which a Surveyor should be employed.

(3) Responsibility for any sewer work (as distinct from the actual house drains or those sewers running along the Estate to the public sewer) for which an expert should be employed.

(4) Responsibility for any forestry work, for which an expert in Forestry should be employed.

But all the above appointments should be made with the understanding that the Consulting Architect, as representing the Trustees, should have the right of supervision, and free inspection at all times, but should not issue any orders or make any alterations in same, without the written consent of the Trustees.

Appendix G

COMPETITION FOR BLOCK PLAN: PRELIMINARY QUESTIONS

1. Whether the Competition shall be 'public' or 'limited'.

2. Whether the Consulting Architect shall be sole Assessor, or whether there shall be two or three Assessors, and, if so, whether one shall be a Surveyor or expert in Forestry. (It appears not to be unusual for a Surveyor to be an Assessor as it is found that Surveyors notice points which Architects may not: an expert in Forestry is suggested by Mr. Cave's admission, in paragraph 19(4) of the Heads of Agreement, that he cannot be responsible for Forestry Work.)

3. Whether each Competitor shall be provided with a reduced scale copy of the Survey and Contour Plan. (This appears to be desirable as the planning of the Burhill Site must depend to a certain extent upon the Contours).
   NB: The Survey and Contour Plan, which is in course of preparation by Messrs. Daniel Smith Son & Oakley, is not expected to be ready before the end of August.

4. What buildings, allotments and amenities are to be provided for in the Plan, viz:

   Whether the Cottages are to be bungalows or two storeyed or part bungalows and part two storeyed.

   Whether they are to be arranged in groups, in pairs, or detached, etc..

   Generally, what are to be the PRINCIPAL FEATURES to be stated in the 'Schedule of Principal Features' attached to the conditions for the Competition.

   The Trustees are reminded that in addition to the Cottages the following buildings, allotments and amenities have from time to time been suggested:

   (1) Administration Block with, or including (if separate buildings):
      (a) Official and Staff Quarters or Residences for Secretaries, Medical Officer, Nurses, Superintendents, Matrons, etc..
      (b) Offices.
   (2) Chapel and Clergy House.
   (3) Cemetery and Mortuary.
   (4) Public Hall, Library, and Club Rooms.
   (5) Common Living Houses with Dining Rooms and Kitchens.
   (6) Cottages of Rest or Infirmary.
   (7) Workshops (including Undertaker's Shop).
   (8) Bakehouse.
   (9) Laundry and Drying Rooms.
   (10) Electric Power Station or Gas Station or both. (The Trustees have to decide what facilities they are going to provide for Lighting, Heating and Cooking.)
   (11) Lodges.
   (12) Stables and Garage.
   (13) Fire Engine Station (if thought necessary).
   (14) Store Houses for Coal etc..
   (15) Shop or Stores.

(16) Memorial to the Founder.
(17) Recreation Ground and Gardens, Bowling Greens, Lawns, etc..

The Trustees are also reminded in this connection that their general opinion is that 500 should be the maximum number of Pensioners, that 7/6d should be the weekly allowance, and that applicants should be chosen irrespective of the question whether or not they are entitled to Old Age Pensions.

5. Whether the Assessor or Assessors shall proceed to draw up the Conditions and Schedule of particulars for the Competition, or whether the Consulting Architect shall first be asked to draw up in conjunction with the Secretary, for consideration by the Trustees, a Schedule of principal features. (This seems to involve to a certain extent crystallising a Scheme for the Homes.)

6. Whether the Competition shall be centralised from the Trustees' Office or from elsewhere. (The former appears to be the more ordinary and convenient course, the Assessors being called in to see the Drawings when all wrappers and marks of identification have been removed.)

20 July 1911.

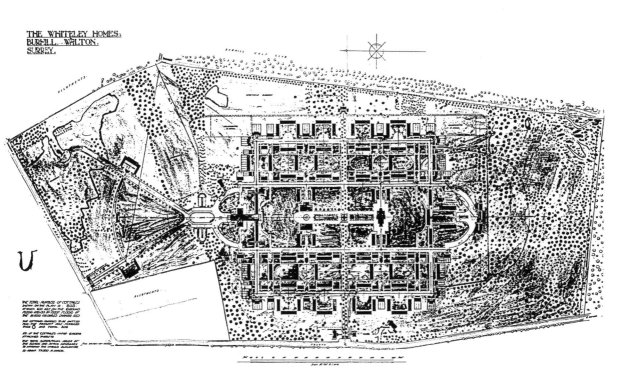

Plan 'U' submitted by Mr Henry T. Hare.

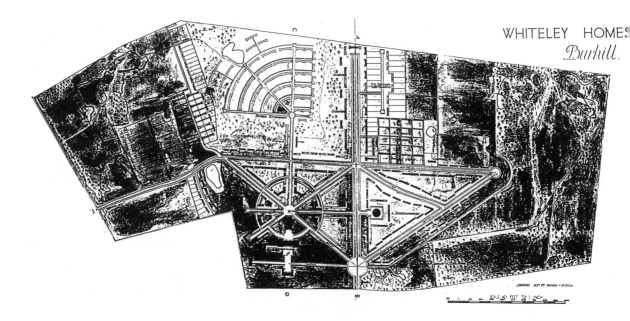

Plan 'V' submitted by Mr Mervyn E. Macartney.

Plan 'W' submitted by Mr R. Frank Atkinson.
WINNER of the FIRST PRIZE.

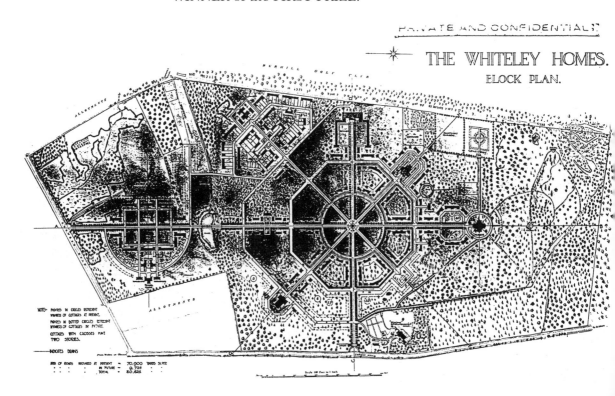

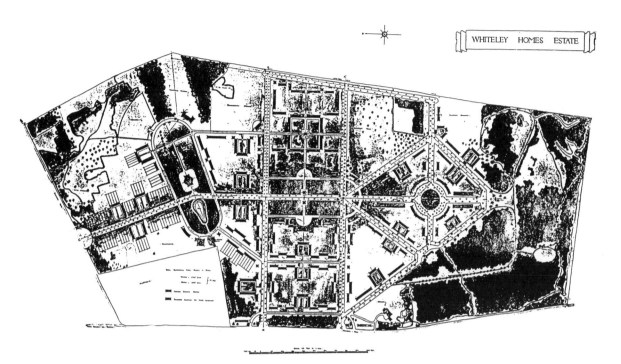

Plan 'X' submitted by Mr Thomas B. Colcutt.
WINNER of the SECOND PRIZE.
Plan 'Z' submitted by Professor Stanley Davenport Adshead, FRIBA.
WINNER of the THIRD PRIZE.

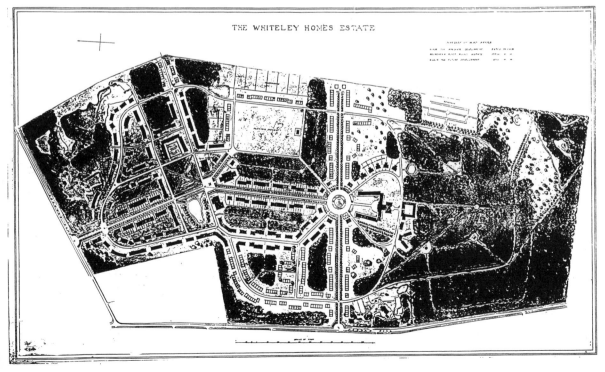

Appendix I

WHITELEY VILLAGE

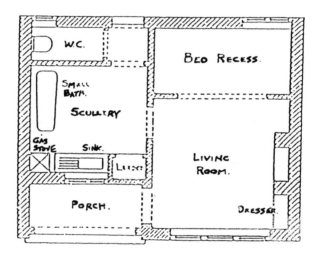

Sketch of the Standard Accommodation
provided in the Single Cottages.
Double Cottages are similar but with larger
Living Room and Bed Recess.

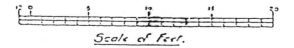

Scale of Feet.

Figures Approximate only.

Section	A. Original design & estimate including oak floors, fittings & external doors, also including provisional amounts for Electric light, Gas Stoves & Meters. (Portland Stone dressing.)	B. Original design & estimate, all as last with oak fitting, but deal floors.	C. Original design & Estimate, but deal floors & fittings, oak external doors remaining. (Deal fittings painted).	D. Original design, but various reductions made in constructions etc to floors & fittings. (Bath Stone.)	E. Alteration to design. Various reductions made in constructions etc., retaining oak fittings, but deal floors and omitting prov. for electric light, gas meters and Cookers. (Bath Stone.)	F. All as last, but deal fittings & floors (Deal painted.) Bath Stone.
No 1. T.Blomfield	£15,485. 4. 3.	£15,075. 2. 0.	£14,086. 3. 7.	£12,922. 4. 3.	£11,235. 0. 0.	£10,246. 0. 0.
2 & 4. E.George	26,799.19. 0.	28,008. 0. 0.	24,504.12. 0.	22,629.19. 0.	20,613. 0. 0.	19,213. 0. 0.
3. E.Newton	15,725. 1.10.	15,417. 6. 7.	14,651.11. 3.	14,487. 0. 0.	12,757. 0. 0.	12,000. 0. 0.
5. M.Macartney	13,578. 4. 7.	13,243. 0. 0.	12,528. 0. 0.	12,185. 4. 7.	11,158. 0. 0.	10,193. 0. 0.
6. Aston Webb	12,442.16. 6.	12,163.12. 0.	11,620.15. 5.	11,349. 0. 0.	10,202. 0. 0.	9,660. 0. 0.
7. F.Atkinson Winner	13,202.19. 0.	12,771.19. 0.	12,025.19. 0.	11,765. 0. 0.	10,506. 0. 0.	9,762. 0. 0.
8. W.Cave	13,009.17. 5.	12,638. 0. 0.	11,549. 0. 0.	11,693. 0. 0.	10,450. 0. 0.	9,550. 0. 0.
	£110,242. 2. 7.	£107,321.19. 7.	£100,966. 1. 3.	£97,036. 7.10.	£96,901. 0. 0.	£80,624. 0. 0.

Appendix K

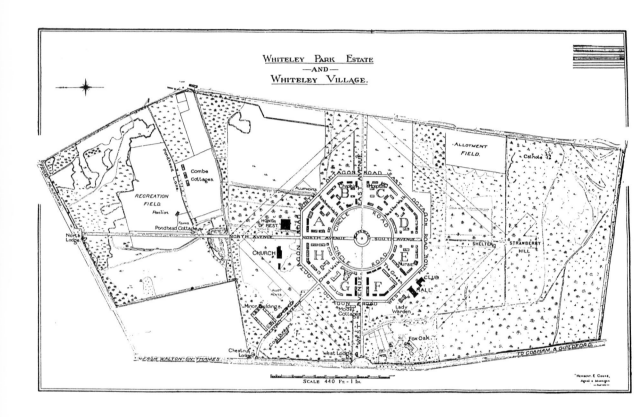

146

Appendix L

Appendix M

Appendix N

Part I
(Published in the January 1949 edition of the village magazine)

Looking back over 31 years, to Whiteley Village in 1917, when there were only 14 Villagers! No roads, avenues or drives were to be seen then; the greens were rough scrub and bracken five feet high.

The first villagers to arrive lived in E and F Sections. Our post office was started by a villager in E Section, No. 18, and the daily papers could be bought at F Section, No. 1. The stores began in the village hall behind the counter where we now serve refreshments. Our stores manageress and the food came from Messrs. William Whiteley's; we were rationed in those days and the delivery of goods was not always on time – sometimes several days late – and we had plenty of grumbles in consequence. The stage in the hall was used as a reading room during the daytime, and we held our first whist drive there with three tables. The centre of the hall was used for church services. The vicar of Hersham held these at 11 o'clock on Sundays, and occasionally took an 8 o'clock celebration. Two ladies from Hersham brought some little girls to sing and afterwards kept them for Sunday School. Sewing meetings also were held in the hall during the week.

The first hospital was started in F Section, No. 4, with one patient. A surgery opened in one room of Nurse's Cottage F Section, and there was also one guest room in the same cottage. The building of the stores and the church was not quite finished, and the kitchen and waiting room were not begun.

Our first transport was called 'the Cart'. This was a covered cart (not nearly so stylish as that now used for removals!), with two long wooden forms holding about ten people. It carried steps to enable villagers to get in and out, much to the amusement of the New Zealand soldiers who were in Walton at that time. Villagers had to put their names down for 'the Cart' and take their turn, as they do today for the bus.

The kitchen was opened in Nurse's Cottage, G Section and the first week or two we served soup only. Meat was not to be had as it was still rationed. The villagers came into residence fairly quickly, and by Christmas there were about thirty. On Christmas Day we had a dinner of turkey, sausages, ham and vegetables. We could not manage a Christmas pudding but had trifle and jelly instead. This dinner was served in some of the empty cottages near the kitchen; trestle tables and chairs were found somewhere, a lovely fire was made in each cottage; the married people were in one house and the single ones in another, and everyone was very happy.

A hand laundry began at Pond Head Cottage (since demolished), and the soiled linen was collected at Section E No. 8, on Thursdays. The milkman and baker came daily, but people had to go to Hersham or Walton to buy meat, the ration being then 1s. 2d. per week.

The village was very rough with no roads made, and everywhere was like the backwoods. One could never imagine that it could look so lovely in a few years. We had about 70 soldiers in the charge of a VC who came to clear some of the paths, and the place began to take shape and to look quite smart. The staff at this time consisted of a village sister and one nurse, a lady gardener, a stores manageress and a cook. The lady warden, Miss Gabbett, lived at Fox Oak.

Anon.

Part II
(Published in the February 1949 edition of the village magazine)

January, 1918 – The weather was very cold and the war was not getting on too well; food was rather short, so it was decided to have some goats to help with the milk supply. The lady gardener was dispatched to the market at Guildford and returned with two goats. She took them for a walk on a chain daily round the village for about a week till they got used to their surroundings. Then they were pegged out on the field at Pond Head where the staff cottages and laundry are today. They slept in sheds at night. In the spring they produced two kids, and who should milk them was the next question. One member of the staff let a word drop that she could milk cows. That was enough: she had the job of milking and selling the milk to villagers. There were more customers than could be supplied as the milk was only about six pints per day, so we decided to let each villager have half-a-pint a day. It was taken round in a large jug and measured. It was rather an amusing job, especially when one customer would say 'you gave me rather short measure yesterday; you'd better give me a little extra today to make that up!' The customer was always right!

In and among this milk business the lady warden expected the goats to be pegged out about twice a day on different patches where they could get more grass in order to increase the milk supply. This was done, but it made little difference to the supply, and we concluded the goats were old and would never give any more whatever happened. It was then decided to have another goat of a better breed, so Guildford market was once again visited, and we bought a lovely young goat called 'Queenie'. She was a little pet, and she cost £10, but quite soon died.

After that we went in for ducks. They looked very nice on the pond and we put a setting down and had several young ones. We did not get as many eggs as we expected; there were a few birds laying but the eggs disappeared, so the ducks were taken to Fox Oak and put in a shed. They were let out each morning for a walk in that lovely fruit and vegetable garden. They soon left their mark on everything in the garden, including the gardener, who saw red every time he saw ducks. We decided to kill a few and have them for dinner in the kitchen, and we felt 'here at last we have produced a meal', much to the delight of the villagers. The remaining ducks were put on the pond.

It was next decided to have rabbits; a meeting was called and a few villagers undertook to look after a hutch at the back of the Sections with a larger hutch at Fox Oak. The villagers looked after them for a time, but some of the rabbits died and so they were all sold, and we were left with just two goats and six ducks. So much for our effort to produce more food!

The lady gardener planted 500 bulbs around the village and although there were not greens or gardens we had lovely spring flowers from the very start. She also drove the pony and trap, and sometimes took the villagers out shopping to Walton or Weybridge.

Anon.

Part III
(Published in the March 1949 edition of the village magazine)

As the population of the village increased, things began to take shape; the church was consecrated by the Bishop of Winchester in April, 1918. It was a very lovely spring day and everyone turned out for the occasion. Church services were then held at 8, 11 and 6.30 o'clock and the Free Church used the hall on Sundays and Wednesdays at 3.30. A library was opened in the hall, and books could be obtained on Wednesday and Saturday afternoons. The milkman arrived in the village each morning at 9.30. The village cart was still the only means of transport – and by special request would leave the monument at 7 o'clock if there was a party of four, to catch the cheap train (1/1 return) to London, calling agin at the station at 4.30 p.m. This was rather early to return, but the villagers were not expected to be out too late in those days!

A lot of our ladies wore bonnets and capes, and the gentlemen top hats and frock-coats (on high days and holidays). The summer was very lovely, and many of the villagers who had come from London or big towns found the country walks (especially the road to Cobham) attractive as the autumn drew near.

More staff arrived – the electrician and his family, and the plumber, too, so we began to settle down. The stores was opened, only part of it being used at first, as the number of customers was still small. Frequently a side of bacon was taken to a shop in Hersham to be sliced; bacon was not rationed at that time!

Our next excitement was the signing of the Armistice. The church bells rang out, and the lady warden (Miss Gabbett) waving a Union Jack, went round the village in a pony trap, driven by Mr. Markey. Thanksgiving prayers were said in the hall at 2 o'clock, and a service in the church the same evening was conducted by the vicar of Hersham.

Section D was opened next, and a night watchman arrived to keep us in order. A cottage hospital was started in Section C with a matron and one nurse in residence. A village nurse helped, also a villager who had been a nurse did duty while some of the others had time off. The villagers were encouraged to help each other as much as possible, especially during illness. The communal kitchen was moved into part of the stores pending a new kitchen being built.

Romances started now. One of the first men to arrive felt rather lonely, and took upon himself to seek a bride. He was unsuccessful in the first six, but the seventh lady, a spinster of 72, said 'yes'. The happy couple were married at Hersham. Most of the villagers went to the church and photographs appeared in the *Daily Mirror* next morning. The honeymoon was spent in Clacton. When they came back they were given a tea party, complete with wedding cake, in the hall. This party also celebrated the golden wedding of two other villagers who looked younger than the newly weds.

Anon.

Part IV (Published in the April 1949 edition of the village magazine)

We had many visits from New Zealand soldiers who were at Mount Felix. They came to play football in the recreation ground. They also gave us concerts and sketches in the hall. After the Armistice they gave us a party, their matron, sisters and nurses, coming with them. They provided all the food and gave us a lovely evening, waiting on the villagers and staff who were all invited by them. We finished up with our first dance.

The guest house was already open, also Section B, with a chaplain in residence there. Our second Christmas was rather different, more people to cater for, and meat still rationed. This time the Trustees gave each villager a dinner, consisting of a pigeon, Christmas pudding, and fruit. The pigeons arrived in a hamper, just as they had been shot, with a couple of crows and a magpie included. The pigeons had to be plucked – a big job as there were about 150 of them – however, they were done in time, and two of us went round the village on Christmas Eve distributing a parcel to each house. After Christmas we had our first Christmas tree and party for the children from Hersham, about 20 coming with the vicar, who helped to entertain them. The villagers had made little gifts and put them on the tree for them.

Our lady warden (Miss Gabbett) needed more help as the village was nearly filled, so her assistant (Mrs. Chapman), came in March 1919. Six months later Miss Gabbett had to resign owing to ill health. Everything which she organised and started is still being carried out today, only on a larger scale. The agent and general manager (Mr. Cooke), came to Fox Oak in May.

About this time a small bus replaced the cart, the chauffeur and his family arriving in Section G. The bus was not very roomy, and soon became known as the Black Maria. The hospital and the Chaplain's house, also the staff houses in Chestnut Avenue began to be built.

The village gates were locked at 10 p.m. and opened at 8 a.m., excepting the workmen's entrance which was open earlier. Anyone out after 10 p.m. had to walk to Fox Oak and come in through the garden and the wood, or to climb the fence.

The kitchen and waiting room were in use by the autumn. The Trustees gave the villagers and staff a Christmas dinner, catered for by Messrs. W. Whiteley and served in the hall. We finished with a Christmas tree and concert.

The last Section (H) was completed about the same time, and was quickly filled – Miss Bishop and Miss Shuter, Miss Elcomb and Mrs. Strode being among those who came into residence then.

Anon.

Appendix O

MEMORANDUM

RECORDING THE FOUNDATION OF THE SCHEME OF THE TRUST

The founder of the Trust was the late William Whiteley of Westbourne Grove, London, whose life story is recorded on the central monument of Whiteley Village. His success in the great business to which he gave his name enhanced by the confidence and co-operation of associates and staff which his genius inspired enabled him to amass the fortune out of which he bequeathed a million sterling for the benefit of the aged poor.

The object of this Memorandum is in the lifetime of some of the original Trustees to place on record for the benefit of future Trustees and others interested the considerations and circumstances which influenced the Trustees in founding the scheme as developed up to the time the village was first opened and other points of interest.

By his Will Mr Whiteley appointed as Trustees the present Chairman Arthur Foley Winnington-Ingram, Lord Bishop of London, Cosmo Gordon Lang, Bishop of Stepney (who retired on preferment to the Archbishopric of York), Charles Henry Mills, Lord Hillingdon (since retired), William Mansfield, Lord Sandhurst (who retired on appointment as Lord Chamberlain), Sir Walpole Greenwell, Bart. (deceased), Mr Whiteley's two sons William and Frank Ernest and William Edward Gillett (his legal adviser).

Mr Whiteley empowered two of the above-named, viz Sir Walpole Greenwell and Mr Gillett to appoint three additional Trustees; and in pursuance of that power, by deed dated the 2nd June 1909, they appointed Col. the Hon. Arthur Grenville Brodrick, Col. Sir Edward Willis Duncan Ward (since retired then permanent Secretary of State for War), and Sir Edward Feetham Coates, Bart MP (deceased).

The body of Trustees so constituted had power under Mr Whiteley's Will by deed to appoint from time to time other additional Trustees, but there were never to be less than two Trustees; and Mr Whiteley expressed the wish that the number should at all times be kept to nine.

By deed of even date with that above mentioned the Trustees appointed Henry Luke Paget, then Bishop of Stepney, who has since retired on preferment to the Bishopric of Chester. By subsequent deeds they appointed William Hayes Fisher, Lord Downham (deceased, then Chairman of the London County Council) and the other Trustees who still hold office.

Of the Trustees who have passed away or resigned the late Sir Walpole Greenwell devoted a very considerable part of his spare time to the affairs of the Trust. A leading stockbroker and a considerable landowner the keenness with which he brought to bear, and gave without stint, the benefit of his experience even on the smallest detail could hardly have been surpassed. If he missed a meeting he felt that he had been out of the battle. Since his death his example has been emulated by Col. the Hon. Arthur Brodrick, the Chairman of the Executive Committee, of whose services the Trustees were deprived while he was serving his country during the war, and through whose kind help the office of the Trust was at the start temporarily accommodated in the Board Room of the Western Telegraph Company, Electra House, Finsbury Pavement, EC.

Throughout the Trustees acted on expert advice. Their first step was to get advice – from Mr Walter Cave, who subsequently acted as consulting architect, and Mr Douglas Eyre, a barrister of standing, who had made a special study of the lives of the poorer classes – as to how the Trustees should exercise the very wide discretion given them by the Founder of the Trust subject to his expressed wish that the homes should be in the western suburbs of London and if possible and convenient within 10 miles from Charing Cross and not on clay soil.

Acting on the reports of these two gentlemen the Trustees applied to the High Court for permission

151

to divide the homes up between different localities; but the court decided that the Founder intended one concentrated memorial. Consequently search was made for a suitable site of sufficient size for the large group of almshouses indicated and this was not likely to be found in a populated district.

After very considerable search and another application to the court resulting in failure to obtain leave to purchase Shirley Park near Croydon – which was suitable in all respects except geographical position – with the assistance of Mr (now Sir) John Oakley of Messrs Daniel Smith Son & Oakley, who subsequently became the consulting surveyor to the Trust, the Trustees found the site at Walton-on-Thames where the homes have been built; and the court sanctioned the purchase although it was outside the 10 mile radius.

The Trustees subsequently purchased the house known as 'Fox Oak' in which they established their administrative headquarters converting part of the house into a boardroom and offices and utilising the remainder as a place of residence for the agent and general manager whom they appointed as their chief official in 1919.

In connection with the foundations of the scheme of the Trust now recorded it has to be borne in mind that they were laid in times just prior to the Great War of 1914-1918 which upset many plans.

Having got their site the Trustees decided on the principle of separate tenements and accessory buildings grouped in the form of a self-contained village in a way best suited to the infirmities of the objects of the charity.

In October 1911 they invited a number of well-known architects in competition to give them ideas as to lay-out, and the following accepted the invitation viz: Messrs Henry T. Hare, R. Frank Atkinson, Thomas E. Colcutt, Mervyn E. Macartney, Stanley D. Adshead and Sir Ernest George.

The lay-out plan selected was that of Mr Frank Atkinson, and it hangs in the London boardroom of the Trust. In its central octagonal features it followed the lines of a sketch Mr Atkinson had some time previously submitted unofficially to Messrs William and Frank Whiteley the sons of the Founder being two of the original Trustees. In addition to the main feature it suggested using for public buildings two spots commanding views – the east end of what is now East Avenue for an administration block and the knoll on which the woodland shelter now stands for the church.

The Trustees were later on to be considering in connection with the higher site between Fox Oak and the present Back Entrance Road an administration block such as Mr Atkinson had contemplated, with wings for hospital and staff quarters, but the idea was set aside.

Having settled the general lay-out the Trustees for their guidance in settling the elevation and accommodation of the cottages in the Octagon erected to the design of Mr Walter Cave the pair of cottages standing at the corner of the Octagon Road and the west end of West Avenue. These were designated 'model cottages', but except on the principle of the greater including the less their accommodation bears no resemblance to that of the villagers' cottages subsequently built. The accommodation was more than old folk could be expected to require or keep clean, and capital cost per head had to be considered.

In April 1913 when the above cottages had been built the Trustees under advice called in selected constructing architects as an alternative to engaging the services of one man or to competitive designs; and thereby achieved the variety of design and harmonious whole which the Octagon and village now present.

The Octagon cottages were divided into eight groups among the architects as follows: Sir Aston Webb, Mr Mervyn Macartney, Sir Ernest George (2 groups), Mr Ernest Newton, Sir Reginald Blomfield, Mr Walter Cave and Mr Frank Atkinson, each architect having half of two octagonal sections so that each architect's group had frontages on the Octagon Road and Circle Road and on either side of one of the Avenues.

The Trustees had previously settled the standard of accommodation to be given in the villagers' cottages by means of rough models set up and furnished by Messrs William Whiteley Limited at their Queen's Road premises.

The arrangement of the cottages decided on was an improvement on the generally obtaining almshouse system which the Trustees had carefully considered: hence a so-called nurse's cottage in each section of the Octagon, but with intercommunication by bell from villager's cottage to nurse's cottage and by telephone from nurse's cottage to 'Fox Oak' – the administrative headquarters. Each nurse's cottage would have a member of the staff – not necessarily a trained nurse – in charge of the section, and there would be expert nurses available and a lady (now called lady warden) over all.

The architects did not quite follow out the Trustees' intention. The nurses' cottages were not uniform in accommodation and in two or three cases not at all what the Trustees had intended. The villagers' cottages had no coal space indoors and the outdoor coal bunkers and dustbins which resulted are in many ways inconvenient for aged persons, and as external features are considered inartistic.

Water lies under parts of the estate in close proximity to the surface, and after some of the cottages had been built additional drainage and pudlo treatment of the basements was found necessary. It is hoped that this will prove entirely effective.

Another item which was the subject of much discussion was the bath and hot water supply, and it was felt that the arrangement of baths in sculleries and hot water geysers might be improved on when more cottages were built.

(It is understood that in some recently built cottages an arrangement is to be found whereby shallow baths are sunk below the floor of the living room and covered with rising flaps close to the fire place so that the cottager can get hot water from the boiler and a bath in warmth. Whether such a device is adapted for old folk is open to question.)

The principle of keeping the village private, and not an open village, was decided on in 1911: hence the ring fence, annual closing of the gates and the agreement with the Walton Urban District Council of the 7th July 1913 under which the Trustees undertake to keep the village roads in repair the council having power to put into operation the Private Street Works Act of 1892.

Subject to the above principle the Trustees wished to encourage visitors to the village under proper regulations with a view to brightening the life of the villagers. In that particular connection they provided a recreation ground where certain sports are now permitted to be carried on by the village staff and authorised clubs.

The village stands on the edge of the geological formation known as Bagshot Sand, and the Trustees were advised to take their water supply from the supply company rather than sink their own wells.

Financially speaking there was little to choose between taking their electric supply in bulk and generating their own, and consequently they decided on the former but to provide accommodation for generating plant.

The question of destroying the village refuse on the spot and of obtaining rebate from the rates in respect of that service was duly considered but was not thought to be practicable.

The Great War of 1914-1918 was an ill wind that blew the Trustees some good, for it compelled them to accumulate income which became available for capital expenditure, and through delay in development caused by the war enabled them to formulate plans for the future on actual experience of the life of the village while only a small part of it was built and available for use.

It enabled them especially to judge of requirements dictated by the comparative isolation of the village. Facilities for religious worship, market stores, communal kitchen, medical and nursing attendance, post office, guest-house, conveyances, entertainments and staff accommodation as they exist today, were all carefully thought out and established to meet this difficulty. What in the case of small groups of almshouses established in populated districts could be got by the inmates within walking distance had of necessity in Whiteley Village to be brought within reach of the inhabitants in spite of the necessarily increased administrative cost.

The north entrance was a difficult problem partly owing to the fall of land on either side of the Entrance Road and partly on account of the angle at which it met the public road. The level and line of the Back Entrance Road (now called Chestnut Avenue) and the relative position of the minor buildings and coal store were also the subject of much deliberation. Except for the above, the deepening and enlargement of the lake and the embankment at the northern end of the North Avenue the road and contract work (other than buildings) did not present more than normal difficulties.

Some interesting ornithological and other occurrences are to be seen in the album now kept at the village of photographs taken at various stages of development.

The Trustees felt that for financial and other reasons a London office was a necessity, imposed by the nature and isolation of the homes. There was also the fact the the Board of Trustees of an undertaking of such magnitude consists of prominent men with other activities whose convenience would have to be studied.

Mr Whiteley gave the Trustees very wide discretionary powers as to the class of person to be relieved and as to the benefits to be provided in conjunction with the homes: and with regard to the latter he enabled them to charge rent, which however has not yet been done. He enjoined them to give preferential consideration to applicants who (or if widows whose husbands) had been engaged in Commercial or Agricultural pursuits.

With the above to guide them the Trustees decided that they would best carry out their Trust by confining its benefits to the deserving better class poor and by fixing the benefits (as they are to-day) on the basis of villagers being assured of a free cottage and a position in which they would have to provide themselves only with food and clothing; and the present 1s. 6d. meal allowance was temporarily provided by way of a bonus addition to a cash allowance of 5s. 0d. a week to ensure their having a certain amount of cooked meals from the village communal kitchen or foodstuff from the market stores.

The Old Age Pension Act of 1908 was not sufficiently generous to make it worth while to insist on applicants relieving the Trust Fund by applying for pension, but the Act of 1919 with its higher rate of pension has since made it possible for the Trustees to effect a considerable saving in respect of the weekly cash allowance; and in cases elected on and after the 27th June 1922 that will be graded according to the villager's private income and Old Age Pension in such a way that each single Villager will be able to count on a minimum weekly cash income of 12s. 6d. and each married villager 10s. 0d.

The Trustees make it a general rule to consider applications on their merits according to priority of application bearing in mind the directions Mr Whiteley has given them as above mentioned. During the war the commercial and agricultural classes suffered less than the professional; consequently the majority of the candidates who came forward and were elected between 1914 and 1918 were not those who came under the preferred categories.

By order of the Trustees.
18th November 1922

ARTHUR D. INGRAM
First Secretary to the Trustees

Appendix P

DEVELOPMENT STATEMENT – 24 JUNE 1922

		Expenditure to 31/12/21	Expenditure in 1922 To-date	Total Expenditure To-date
1.	Preliminary: Survey plan & expenses	1,080 10 5		1,080 10 5
2.	Consultants and other expert fees	12,494 12 6		12,494 12 6
3.	Preparing and clearing the land inc. purchase of Forestry Tools	11,283 5 9½		11,283 5 9½
4.	Hire & rolling stock	903 18 10		903 18 10
5.	Laying out of grounds	4,403 6 1½	1,045 13 6	5,335 10 6½
6.	Park-keepers' wages	312 10 3		312 10 3
7.	General Foreman	126 12 –		126 12 –
8.	Roads and Services	98,559 17 4	605 11 8	99,165 9 –
9.	Road Lighting	80 – –		80 – –
10.	Lake	935 3 3		935 3 3
11.	Laying out of Greenswards	355 10 8	620 8 7	975 19 3
12.	Fencing round Park	1,923 16 7		1,923 16 7
13.	Recreation Ground	1,871 4 8½		1,871 4 8½
14.	Seats for Grounds	42 3 8	2 18	42 3 8
15.	Buildings less Government grant = £1560	228,886 4 4	7,485 1 7	229,282 11 4
16.	Market Stores & Kitchen equipment	419 15 4½		419 15 4½
17.	Coal Bunkers	621 7 8		621 7 8
18.	Pit for weighing Machine	48 17 4		48 17 4
19.	Water Mains – Fire appliances	5,248 5 8		5,248 5 8
20.	Electric Mains	9,630 19 1		9,630 19 11
21.	Gas Mains	3,997 15 7	43 13 2	4,041 8 9
22.	Sub Station	43 14 –		43 14 –
23.	Telephone Installation	814 – 8	4 18 4	818 19 –
24.	Electrical General Expenses	553 8 9		553 8 9
25.	Switchboard & Misc. instruments	385 17 1		385 17 1
26.	Furniture – Model Cottages	45 6 2		45 6 2
27.	Hall Clock and bells	231 17 6		231 17 6
28.	Furniture – Cottages etc	8,749 5 10½	156 18 2	8,893 7 –½
29.	Library	125 16 2		125 16 2
30.	Cinematograph	314 16 6½		314 16 6½
31.	Medical Accessories	52 9 6		52 9 6
32.	Tools & Implements	1,677 16 –	101 10 –	1,779 6 –
33.	Fox Oak – General Expenditure	4,185 13 –½		4,185 13 –½
34.	Pond–head Cottage – repairs	122 19 –		122 19 –
35.	Travelling expenses and sundries	2,019 15 1½	19 1 9	2,038 16 10½
36.	Independent Medical Reports	223 13 –		223 13 –

	Expenditure to 31/12/21	Expenditure in 1922 To-date	Total Expenditure To-date
37. Coal Scoop & Sack	34 19 1		34 19 1
38. Motor Vehicles for Village	2,146 8 –		2,146 8 –
39. Flag Staff	154 18 –		154 18 –
40. Fencing round Horse Meadow		35 – 6	35 – 6
Totals	405,108 11	610,120 15 3	415,329 6 9

Cost of land being developed

Main Site	40,714 14 8
Fox Oak	7,185 13 4
Total	47,900 8 –

Appendix Q

WHITELEY HOMES TRUST

HOME OF REST.

TIME TABLE FOR VILLAGERS IN REST HOMES.

7 a.m.	Called with Cup of Tea.
8.30 a.m.	Breakfast in Dining Room.
12.15 p.m.	Dinner in Dining Room.
4 p.m.	Tea in Dining Room.
7 p.m.	Supper in Own Room.
10 p.m.	In bed, and lights out.

N.B. All meals, except Supper, to be taken in the Dining Room.

Ablutions in Bath Room.

Rooms to be dusted and kept tidy.

All cases of illness to be nursed in Hospital.

BY ORDER OF THE TRUSTEES.

FURNITURE FOR REST ROOM

Single Room		Double
Easy chair	1	2
Small chairs	3	4
Chest of Drawers	1	1
Table	1	1
Bedside table or		
Locker	1	1
Coal box	1	1
Fender & Fireirons		
China & ornaments	6	8
Pictures	6	8
Clock		
Carpet & 2 rugs		
Sofa with Matron's permission		
Suit cases & trunks kept in box room		

BY ORDER OF THE TRUSTEES

157

Appendix R

RECOLLECTIONS OF WHITELEY VILLAGE IN 1934 WRITTEN BY MRS MUNDY IN 1988

Biographical Note:
Mrs. Mundy came to work in the village hospital as a nurse in September 1934, and stayed until January 1936. She returned to the village in October 1944, and ran the guest-house until she again left in April 1949 to marry Mr. Charles Mundy, whose parents had been villagers. They both returned to the village as villagers in December 1967. Sadly, he died soon afterwards in April 1969. In February 1986 Mrs. Mundy moved into a room in Whiteley House.

My first recollection of Whiteley Village was of a beautiful estate surrounded by trees and shrubs.

At one end was a pond with a bridge and as you walked on up to the centre of the village was a statue of William Whiteley.

The hospital I came to in 1934 was fully staffed with a matron who had her own quarters in the hospital, and the three sisters who lived in 'nice' rooms in the nurses' home joining the hospital – at that time the verandah at one side of the hospital was made of wood and all open (the patients sat out in the summer) and at one end there was a very large ice box to keep the patients' butter, milk, etc.

Many years before that they had a nice large cottage for a district nurse for the villagers. Then when the hospital was built they had bells in the cottages to ring for help and in each section the bells were put into a staff cottage where the villagers could ring to, and that person would go and see if they could help and if they could not, went down to the hospital for a sister to come and see them.

Small details. The pillar box outside the stores was painted green. A big kitchen near to the stores provided dinners, with two free dinners a week. I think the villagers paid eight pence (in old money) and all had a dinner can. Also villagers were given a bag of coal each week and at Christmas time a large bag of logs for everyone.

Lights had to be out at 10 p.m. – one of the staff had to go round to check and of course if you did have one on they would knock and remind you. In the winter they had a play every Saturday night in the hall and also Tuesday nights they had a film.

Regarding transport, we only had one large bus and also a big old Daimler car and one of the drivers (in the summer) used to take four patients in Whiteley House for a drive on Wednesday afternoons. Later we had another van to take more villagers into the town. It looked just like a prison van; no side windows and we had to get out at the back, but at the time it did help more people to get out.

Appendix S

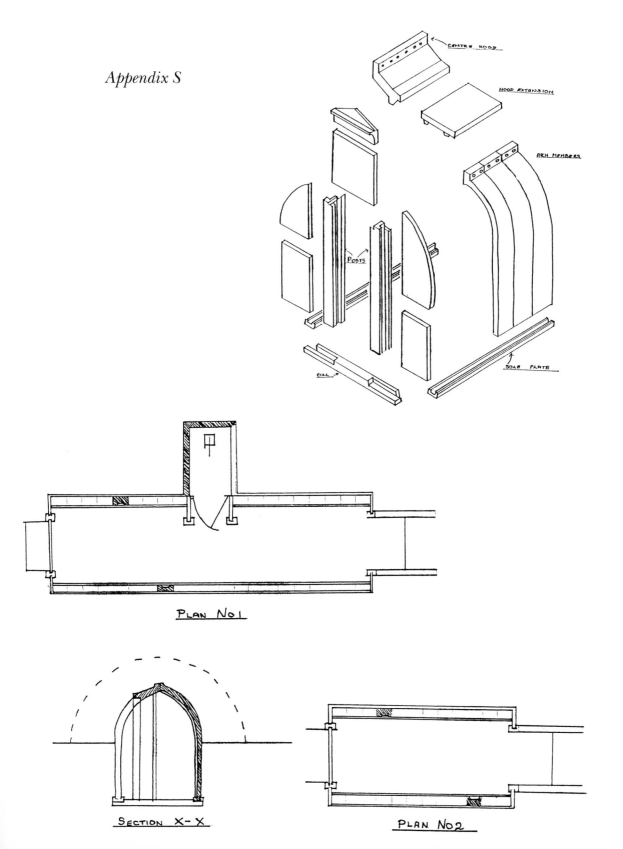

CENTRE HOOD

HOOD EXTENSION

ARCH MEMBERS

POSTS

CILL

SOLE PLATE

PLAN No I

SECTION X - X

PLAN No 2

Appendix T

WHITELEY VILLAGE 'FARM'

There is surprisingly little in the village records in the way of solid information about the 'farm'. What does exist generally refers to farm accounts and livestock or equipment transactions (once again illustrating that the Trustees' minutes were not written with historical researchers in mind!).

However, it is possible to put a few details together and get a rough picture of the Whiteley Village 'farm'.

Calling it a 'farm' is, arguably, a bit of a misnomer – it was more of a market garden than anything else. There does not seem to have been any conscious decision on the part of the Trustees to start a farm on the estate as part of the village amenities; rather, the farm appeared to grow and develop in parallel with the needs of the village.

Crops were being grown at the village before the villagers arrived – presumably this was due to circumstances in the wider world, i.e. the great war of 1914-18. It is more than likely that the Trustees, like other landowners, were encouraged to put what land they could to good use by growing vegetables for the war effort. When the villagers began to arrive in late 1917, there was already a source of fresh, cheap vegetables at a time when supplies were still scarce. The Trustees were quick to see the advantages of supplying the village with 'fresh vegetables at Covent Garden prices' (ie. no middle man!).

Potatoes always made up a large part of the total output of the farm, but other vegetables and a few crops were grown too. A few horses were kept on the estate, and these were fed with home-grown Whiteley Village oats.

The main area where these vegetables were grown was an area of land due east of the hospital, and to the north-eastern end of Hornbeam Walk (where the allotments and rugby field are today). Other areas of the estate seem to have been used for cultivation at various times in the history of Whiteley Village. The land on the north-western corner of the estate that was acquired in the 1930s from the Trustees of Walton's Poor Land (known as 'High Park') was used from the late 1930s until well after the war. During the war itself, an extra section of High Park was cleared of trees and ploughed up as well as an area of the recreation ground.

The Second World War years were probably the most productive for the village farm – villagers were rarely short of vegetables, in fact enough potatoes were grown to supply the hospital kitchen, the communal kitchen and the village stores throughout the war.

Some livestock was kept on the estate; a few horses, goats (for milk) and pigs. There was occasional talk over the years about increasing the amount of livestock kept on the estate to include chickens, dairy cows and sheep, but without result.

The idea of keeping pigs on the estate goes back to 1916 when the Trustees were discussing waste disposal from the village and trying to come to some arrangement with Walton Council regarding this matter. It was suggested that having pigs on the estate would be an effective way of dealing with waste food which would probably form a large proportion of village waste, leaving what was left to be taken away by the local authority. The principle of keeping pigs was adopted in 1916 but not put into practice until early 1918 when Miss Gabbett bought some pigs to deal with the waste from the newly established communal kitchen. Initially, Miss Gabbett was also responsible for the welfare of the pigs, but the Trustees quickly decided that this was not a proper job for a lady – let alone their lady warden – and one of the estate labourers was instructed to take over.

'The Piggeries' were situated behind Pondhead Cottage (about due south) and just east of the pond itself. The pigs, as well as using up waste food from the village, also provided an occasional supply of bacon and a small income – pigs bred on the estate were regularly sold at Kingston market.

The farm continued to grow vegetables and keep pigs for a number of years after the war, but there are fewer references made to it in the Trustees' minutes – the last reference to be found is in July 1968, a reference to the proposed rewiring of the farm buildings.

160

Appendix U

LOCATION LOAF

¾ lb. sausage meat
Pepper and salt
4 oz. stale bread (soaked in cold water)
5 oz. haricot beans (white or coloured)
1 teaspoonful thyme or mixed herbs
Browning

Soak beans overnight. Cook until tender. Squeeze bread to remove moisture and mix with the cooked beans, sausage and seasonings. Make the mixture a rich colour with gravy browning. Press into a greased tin (cocoa tin, 1-lb size, or long tin) and steam for two hours. Then roll in browned crumbs and serve cold with cabbage salad and boiled potatoes. If desired hot, serve with a brown gravy.

ROLY POLY (Sweet)

6 oz. national flour
1 teaspoonful baking powder
1 oz. suet
Pinch of salt
1 oz. grated raw potato
Water to mix
Jam, treacle or fruit to choice

Rub the fat into the flour, add the baking powder, salt and grated raw potato. Mix to a stiff dough with cold water (it might take a little more water than usual). Roll out, and your dough is ready.

Spread jam, treacle or fruit on your rolled-out dough, roll up as usual and either steam it for an hour and a half, or bake it in a moderate oven for 40 minutes to 1 hour. If you are steaming, wrap the pudding in a floured cloth. If you are baking, roll it in oatmeal. You will find the oatmeal will toast a most succulent brown.

FARMHOUSE PASTY

8 oz. national flour
2 oz. fat
4 oz. mashed potatoes
Salt

Make pastry in the usual way, cut into two, roll out one half and line a tin plate with it. Keep the other bit for the lid. Fill it with about 6 ounces of the American pork sausage meat, or some rashers of bacon if you like, and stuffing.

STUFFING 2 teacupfuls wheatmeal breadcrumbs
½ lb. mixed vegetables (including some leek or onion if possible)
2 teaspoonfuls sage
Salt and pepper, a dash of mustard, ground cloves if you like
Vegetable water

Mix the stuffing to a stiffish paste with the vegetable water, and cut into slices. Have your meat in slices too. Then fill the plate you lined with pastry, putting meat and stuffing in layers. Pile it up – these quantities make a good fat pie. Roll out your second bit of pastry, fit it on the top of the pie, make a hole in the middle and decorate it with the trimmings. Bake in a good oven for about half an hour.

1740 PUDDING (Old English Recipe)

1 cupful grated raw carrot
½ cupful raisins
1 cupful grated raw potato
1 teaspoonful bicarbonate soda
1 cupful flour
½ cupful sugar
1 teaspoon nutmeg
1 teaspoonful mixed spice

Mix the grated vegetables with the sugar. Sift together the dry ingredients, add the raisins. Mix thoroughly and stir into the vegetables and sugar. Put into a well-greased basin or mould, cover and steam for 4 hours.

Appendix V

THOUGHTS OF A 'WV' FIRE WATCHER

Printed in the Whiteley Village Magazine, October 1942

My night up. Fire Watching!! Duty Nights seem to come round quickly, although only one in six, apart from turning out when 'They are about'.

2 am. Tired of reading, decide to go outside cottage and look round Section. Everything very quiet, wonderful early-morning crisp air, livens one up. Moon shining through very slowly moving cloud, light and fleecy; looks very beautiful. Village a picture in the moonlight. Tread quietly, not to waken anyone up. Walking on the gravel paths sounds so heavy when everything is still. Wonder if the Villagers ever think of Fire Watchers and Staff on duty when they themselves are having, I hope, a good night's rest. After about twenty minutes outside, feeling fresher and more alert, return to cottage for another reading spell.

4 am. I go outside again, sit on the Bunker for a while and 'think things'. Nearby owl in the Woods is making a noise. Feeling tired, so get inide home again, shall not be sorry when time comes to 'knock off'. Glad it has been so far a quiet night. Think also of the other old Villagers on duty, doing their turn at Fire Watching. Wonder also if their long sit-up-hours are appreciated. Console myself that some of us old ones, able and anxious to do 'our bit', are at least trying to help, and hope that Whiteley Village, will escape trouble – and so, in time, to bed. 'Good night' no 'Good morning'!!

F

INSCRIPTIONS ON THE MEMORIAL TABLETS IN ST. MARK'S CHURCH, WHITELEY VILLAGE

TO THE MEMORY OF
THE RIGHT REVEREND
AND RIGHT HONOURABLE
ARTHUR FOLEY WINNINGTON-INGRAM
WHO IN 1907 BECAME THE FIRST CHAIRMAN OF
THE WHITELEY HOMES TRUSTEES AND RETAINED
THAT OFFICE UNTIL HIS DEATH IN 1946
He loved life and saw good days

IN MEMORY OF
Sgt. **GEORGE KING**
AND
L/Bdr **JOHN WALLACE**
BOTH OF THE ROYAL ARTILLERY
MEMBERS OF THE STAFF OF THIS VILLAGE
WHO DIED WHILE PRISONERS OF WAR
IN THE HANDS OF THE JAPANESE
1943
Their name Liveth

IN MEMORY OF **ALEC GEORGE MOODY** AGED 33
OF THIS VILLAGE, WHO LOST HIS LIFE IN A
GALLANT EFFORT TO SAVE HIS YOUNG COMPANION
GORDON CHARLES MAYNARD AGED 10
WHO WAS DROWNED IN THE RIVER MOLE
IN BURHILL PARK ON 30TH JUNE 1946
Greater love hath no man than this

IN MEMORY OF
W/Off. **JOHN NORMAN MESSENGER**
ROYAL AIR FORCE
OF THIS VILLAGE, WHO WAS KILLED IN ITALY
ON 15TH DECEMBER 1944
They shall mount with wings

Appendix X

INCOME & EXPENDITURE (1948-68)

| | EXCESS OF: | | | EXCESS OF: | |
	INC/EXP	EXP/INC		INC/EXP	EXP/INC
1948	937	–	1960	3,106	–
1949	–	1,907	1961	–	2,707
1950	–	1,155	1962	741	–
1951	–	2,342	1963	1,661	–
1952	–	3,099	1964	9,608	–
1953	–	2,684	1965	12,717	–
1954	–	1,697	1966	7,626	–
1955	2,073	–	1967	5,197	–
1956	1,300	–	1968	–	11,610
1957	644	–	–	–	–
1958	–	5,921	–	–	–
1959	–	2,623			

Appendix Y

TABLE OF WEEKLY COTTAGE AMENITY CHARGES

DATE FROM	REVISED RATE		DATE FROM	REVISED RATE	
	SINGLE	DOUBLE		SINGLE	DOUBLE
03.07.50	12½p	18p	04.05.75	6.37	9.94
01.02.54*	50p	75p	17.11.75***	6.37	9.94
01.04.56	50p	75p	13.06.76	8.33	12.04
06.10.59	62½p	90p	31.07.77	9.31	13.51
03.04.61	72p	1.16	06.08.78	10.99	16.24
26.05.63	87p	1.40	24.08.80	13.51	19.53
20.10.64**	75p	1.28	05.07.81	16.24	23.45
29.03.65	1.02	1.63	24.07.83	19.67	28.35
24.10.67	1.13	1.83	01.07.84	21.00	30.10
16.11.69	2.73	4.34	01.07.85	22.05	31.64
31.10.71	3.43	5.39	01.07.86	23.45	33.46
15.07.73	4.27	6.65	01.07.87	25.13	35.14
21.07.74	5.11	7.98			

NOTES:

RATES applicable prior to decimalisation have been converted to decimal sums.

*　　Only applicable to new Villagers until 1 April 1956.

**　　Villagers now paid for their own electricity. (This did not include night storage heating, as they still had coal fires).

***　　From 17.11.85 Villagers became responsible for paying their own electric night storage heating costs.

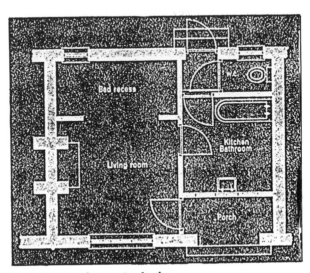

Typical plan before modernisation

COTTAGE MODERNISATION PLANS

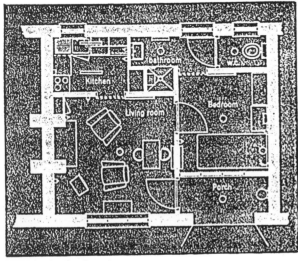

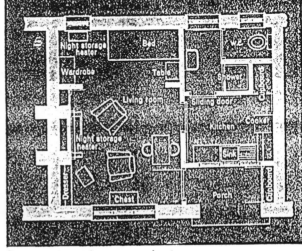

First modernisation plan

Second revised scheme for modernisation

Appendix AA

STATEMENT OF COSTS OF COTTAGE MODERNISATION

Section	Approx. Estimate (£)	Final Cost (£)	On Approx. Estimate		Grant (£)	Final Cost to Trust (£)
			Saving (£)	Addition (£)		
A	49,800	49,263	537	–	6,157	43,106
B	51,460	49,478	1,982	–	7,009	42,469
C	46,545	46,216	329	–	6,442	39,774
D	49,755	53,535	–	3,780	6,915	46,620
E	46,545	50,475	–	3,930	6,590	43,885
F	51,360	56,055	–	–	8,042	–
G	46,545	49,433	–	2,888	6,526	42,907
H	51,360	55,158	–	3,798	7,700	47,458
J	25,680	27,156	–	1,476	3,380	23,776
TOTALS	419,050	436,769	2,848	15,872	58,761	329,995

NOTES:

Figures for A Section include cottage A5

Figures for G Section include conversion of G Section Staff house into three cottages.

Expenditure for F Section includes cost of alterations to F Section Staff House which were not included in approximate estimate.

Final costs for D Section include alterations to 39 and 39a Circle Road which were not included in the approximate estimate.

Final costs for H Section include the sum of £1,184 due to SEEBOARD and not yet paid.

Final costs for E Section include the total of £1,035 due to SEEBOARD and not yet paid.

INDEX

(Compiled by Auriol Griffith-Jones)